The
Brahmo Samaj & Arya Samaj
in their bearing upon Christianity

The Brahmo Samaj & Arya Samaj

in their bearing upon Christianity

A Study in Indian Theism

BY

Frank Lillingston, M.A.

GYAN

Published by

Gyan Publishing House
5, Ansari Road
Daryaganj, New Delhi-110002
Phone: 011-47034999, 9811692060
E-mail: books@gyanbooks.com

Distribution Network
gyanbooks.com
India, USA, Canada, UK, Australia

ISBN: 978-93-6208-190-2 (PB)
First Published, 1901

2nd Impression 2024

Printed at: Gyan Press, Delhi.

THE BRAHMO SAMAJ & ARYA SAMAJ IN THEIR BEARING UPON CHRISTIANITY

Author: FRANK LILLINGSTON

THE BRAHMO SAMAJ AND ARYA SAMAJ

The Brahmo Samaj & Arya Samaj in their bearing upon Christianity

A Study in Indian Theism

By

Frank Lillingston, M.A.

Assistant Curate of Heavitree, Exeter
Formerly Scholar of Pembroke College, and Lecturer in Hebrew
and O.T. History at Selwyn College, Cambridge

London
Macmillan and Co., Limited
New York: The Macmillan Company
1901

TO THE

CAMBRIDGE BROTHERHOOD

IN DELHI.

PREFACE

> "Forgive them where they fail in truth,
> And in Thy wisdom make me wise."

THE purpose of this small book is two-fold. First; I have attempted to give a short historical sketch of the development in the past of monotheistic thought in India. Secondly; I have sought to compare, or to contrast, this monotheism, at its various stages, with the monotheism of Christianity. To do this involves enquiry into the most profound religious questions, enquiry which it is quite beyond the scope of this work to pursue in detail, and yet it is hoped that the short summaries of Christian doctrine given below may be suggestive of lines of thought, which the marginal references to authorities may enable the reader to verify, develop, and, perhaps, make his own. The work is dedicated to Christian Missionaries; may it be to them fresh proof that they, in their arduous and noble work, have the support of the sympathy in thought and prayer of the Church at home.

Should these pages come before the notice of members of those Societies, whose doctrines I have attempted to delineate and to criticise, I would ask them to see in the words of our great English Poet, which stand at the beginning of this Preface, the Spirit in which it has been my earnest effort to write this essay; may they in their counter-criticism effect the purpose which is our common aim, the removal of error and the exaltation of Truth.

The interchange of thought between England and India is in these days so rapid that we in both countries have to face the same questions. It is my hope therefore that this little book may serve the purpose of an index,—it cannot claim to be more,—to Christian lines of thought for those in this country who feel the need to give a reason for the hope that is in them.

My acknowledgments are due to the many friends who have assisted me in my task by the generous loan of books, and by friendly criticism.

FRANK LILLINGSTON.

HEAVITREE,
May 13, 1901.

LIST OF WORKS ON INDIAN THEISM REFERRED TO BELOW.

Wilson, H. H. *Essays and Lectures on the Religion of the Hindus.* Vols. I. and II. (1861).

Williams, Sir M. Monier. *Hinduism.* S.P.C.K. *Non-Christian Religious Systems.*

Williams, Sir M. Monier. *Indian Wisdom.*

Williams, Sir M. Monier. *Religious Thought and Life in India.*

Williams, Sir M. Monier, in the *Journal of the Royal Asiatic Society,* Jan.—April, 1881.

Williams, Sir M. Monier. *Modern India.*

Hopkins, Prof. E. W. *The Religions of India.* Arnold, 1896.

Barth, Prof. A. *The Religions of India.* Trübner and Co., 1891.

Davids, Prof. Rhys. *Hibbert Lecture,* 1881.

Ellinwood. *Oriental Religions and Christianity.*

Lyall, Sir A. C. *Asiatic Studies,* 1882. (First Series.)

Lyall, Sir A. C. *Asiatic Studies,* 1889. (Second Series.)

Robson. *Hinduism, its relations to Christianity.*

Carpenter, Mary. *Last days in England of Rammohun Roy.*

Rammohun Roy. *Second Appeal* and *Final Appeal.*

Collet, Miss S. D. *Brahmo Year Books, 1876-82.*

Brahmo Tract Society, Calcutta. *Keshab Chander Sen in England.* Vols. I. and II.

Mozoomdar Pertab Chunder. *Faith and Progress of the Brahmo Somaj.* Calcutta, 1882.

Slater, T. E. *Keshab Chander Sen, the Brahmo Samaj.* Madras, 1884.

Bhattacharjee, J. N. *Hindu Castes and Sects.* Calcutta, 1896.

Williams, T. *Exposure of Dayananda Sarasvati.* Delhi, 1889.

Müller, Prof. Max. *The Vedanta Philosophy.*

Müller, Prof. Max. *Biographical Essays,—Dayananda Sarasvati* (cit. Oman).

Müller, Prof. Max. *Sacred Books of the East.* Vol I. *The Upanishads.*

Westcott, Bp., in *Cambridge Companion to the Bible*, 1893.

Encyclopædia Britannica (9th Edition). *Brahmo Somaj.*

Encyclopædia Britannica (9th Edition). *Hindustani Literature.*

Encyclopædia Britannica (9th Edition). *Vedanta.*

Encyclopædia Britannica (9th Edition). *Brahmanism.*

Cambridge Mission to Delhi. *Annual Reports for 1898-9.*

Cambridge Mission to Delhi. *Occasional Paper No. 15.*

Longridge, J. *The Oxford Mission to Calcutta.* 1900.

Society for the Propagation of the Gospel. *Digest of Records, 1701-1892.*

Oman, Prof. J. Campbell. *Indian Life: Religious and Social.*

Clark, Dr. Martyn. *The Principles and Teaching of the Arya Samaj.* Lahore, 1886-7.

Christian Literature Society for India. *The Brahma Samajes.*

Christian Literature Society for India. *Defectiveness of Brahmoism.*

CONTENTS

Ὁ Λόγος σὰρξ ἐγένετο.

INTRODUCTORY.

"LET India accept Christ," were the words of Keshab Chunder Sen, one of the leaders of the Brahmo Samaj of India, when he preached to a large congregation at Calcutta in 1879. To Christian ears no words could be more welcome; the blood of Christian martyrs, the seed of the Church, seems at first sight to have taken root in the soil of India, when Christ is preached not only by foreigners, but by many of her own sons. The impulse of Christians is to welcome these Reformers of the Faiths of India as fellow-workers in the service of Christ, and to look for far greater results from their preaching than can ever come from the stammering lips of Europeans. But before we turn from India to concentrate our forces upon the work to be done in other lands, we need the assurance that the torch has been really kindled in India; we cannot be satisfied with a flicker of light that perchance is only borrowed; before the Holy Catholic Church can regard the Brahmo-

Samaj, the Arya-Samaj, or any other Samaj as its fellow-labourer and successor in this work, it must satisfy itself that the essential truths of the Historic Faith will be handed down to generations to come. The need of such careful inquiry into the nature of these claimants to the title of Christian has been impressed upon us by the experience of the years that have elapsed since the words of Keshab Chunder Sen, quoted above, were uttered. The Oxford University Mission in Calcutta owes its origin to the approximation of the teaching of the Brahmo-Samaj to Christianity;[1] but its members are said to have found that the aim of Keshab Chunder Sen was something quite different from discipleship of Christ.[2] We welcome indeed the fresh light which contact with Indian wisdom throws upon our faith, bringing out its beauty with fresh brilliancy, and, as we believe, making it the more acceptable to Indian minds, but we still "hold fast that which is true," accounting ourselves the best judges of the value and truth of that which has been our possession for countless generations, and not listening to the childish impatience which bids us cast away the truths which it has not yet learnt to understand; we believe that the time will come when the Church

[1] *The Oxford Mission to Calcutta*, pp. 1 and 2.

[2] *Guardian*, June 27, 1900, p. 934. Speech by Canon Gore.

of India, rich in the possession of the best fruits of Eastern and Western thought, will thank God for preserving to her an Historic Faith which takes account of things subjective and things objective, spiritual and material, of thought and action, a Faith which satisfies men of every type of character because it answers to the fulness of Life.

In the present essay both the Brahmo and Arya Samaj are examined from the standpoint of one who has accepted the teaching of the Catholic Church with regard to the Blessed Trinity, as expressed in the so-called Creed of Athanasius, as true. That is to say, he believes in the Unity of the Nature of God and in the Tri-personality within the one Nature. Jesus Christ is to him at once true man and true God; His relationship to God is unique:[1] it is not the same as that of any other man to the Father.

Such a standpoint is not popular in these days, when it is recognised that free unbiassed enquiry is essential to the discovery of truth, and yet it is by no means indefensible. For, supposing we assume that the teaching of the Catholic Church is, so far as it goes, absolute truth, a not impossible assumption, it will follow that to be able rightly

[1] See Lightfoot on meaning of μονογένης. *Clem. Rom. to Corinthians*, Large Ed., p. 87. Cit. Rashdall, *Doctrine and Development*, pp. 77 *sq.*

to appreciate other creeds, they must be viewed from the Christian standpoint; upon this assumption every enquirer who is not a Christian is in partial darkness, and his judgment is so biassed that he cannot hope to form any sound judgment upon the subject of his enquiry.[1] Yet this assumption is one that will be made only by those who have not learnt, and refuse to learn, to apply the methods of historical criticism and inductive reasoning to Christianity as to any other religion. We have no intention of adopting such an attitude. To us belief in the absolute truth of Christianity is not an assumption, but may be arrived at as the result of a process of inductive reasoning, under certain moral conditions. We hold that so far as the truth of the Creed of the Christian Church is called in question, it is right that every fact upon which that Creed is based should be laid open to the enquirer that he may be able, by the accumulation of evidence under his own eyes, to judge whether it, when summed up, does or does not shape itself into a conclusion identical with the Christian Creed. And yet further, we are prepared to add to the evidences before us any fresh ones that may be produced in the course of time, as for instance such fresh light as has been given to us through the recognition of the

[1] Thus Tertullian, *de præscript*: 3, 'Nemo sapiens est, nisi fidelis.'

principle of evolution. We believe it to be quite possible that such new evidence may demand the insertion of new, supplementary but not contradictory, clauses within the creed in order to give expression to a more enlightened faith; and we also think it possible that fresh evidence may make it expedient for us to alter the wording of our creed, in order that its language may keep pace with the growth in meaning of the truths it conveys, instead of leading to the stagnation of thought.[1] In the case, however, of the enquiry now before us into the teaching of the Brahmo and Arya Samaj and their bearing on Christianity, we deliberately follow the deductive rather than the inductive method for these reasons. The Christian Creed is already accepted by us on grounds of inductive reasoning so far as its facts as facts are concerned:[2] we need not, therefore, repeat this process unless anything of the nature of fresh evidence be laid before us: now in the present case those who have criticised the Brahmo and Arya Samaj from a purely historical standpoint give us to understand that the principles

[1] Westcott, *Gospel of Life*, p. 281, "We cannot believe what was believed in another age by repeating the formulas which were then current." We think the term 'Hades' would, in the English translation of the Nicene creed, be preferable to 'Hell.'

[2] Though we grant that these facts can be fully apprehended only through the exercise of the spiritual faculty. Westcott, *Ibid.*, p. 81.

upon which these societies rest are in no sense new,[1] they are the same principles that have in the past been examined in their relation to Christianity, and, on grounds that satisfy us, have been rejected: a fresh investigation, in accordance with the rules of induction, of the respective claims of Indian Theism (so far as it is pure Theism) and Catholic Trinitarianism might be of interest on account of the introduction of new terminology which it would involve, but beyond this we think it would be of little value, for the arguments adduced would be only those of former times. We maintain that more will be gained by the inversion of the process, and the examination of the principles of the two Samaj, and of their relationship to Christianity, by methods of deduction from the accepted belief of the Christian Church. We shall not, it is true, be placing ourselves in the thrilling and dramatic position of those who are still at liberty to choose between the acceptance of two opposing faiths: ours is a more prosaic attitude; to us it seems that inductive reasoning has had

[1] M. Williams, *Indian Theistic Reformers* (Royal Asiatic Society), p. 1. Hopkins, p. 515, 'modern Deism not the result of new influences.' Barth, p. 220, 291.

On the other hand see *Indian Theistic Reformers*, p. 11, 'A new phase of the Hindu religion differing essentially from every other.' The combinations of Eastern and Western thought, new to India in the 19th century, had affected Europe in the 3rd century, the burden of re-sifting evidence therefore rests with Hindus, not with Christians.

its scope, it has done its work, we accept its conclusions, and now proceed to use these as the test of the value of others which have no independent evidence in their favour. That historical evidence which was formerly regarded as the foundation upon which our present structure was to be reared now appears in a new light as illustrative of our creed and as a subsidiary proof of its truth. It is true that the value of such an enquiry into the history of a belief other than our own, will still depend upon the correctness of the conclusions which we have come to by inductive reasoning; but this deductive method which we adopt will give us sympathy with the weakness and the strength of the objects of our enquiry, such as the other could not offer, for the method of deduction is after all more closely in correspondence with the progress of life: man learns truth by collecting facts and from them drawing his conclusions; God makes truth, causing all things to issue from the one source; we can best hope to understand truth when we view history and the thoughts of men from the standpoint of the knowledge of their Maker, and in their relation to Him, tracing the gradual development of belief from the past to the present, rather than from the present to the past.

The character of the Brahmo and Arya Samaj

in their earlier history and later developments can be justly estimated only by those who know something of the religious soil from whence they sprung, and of the religious movements which preceded them. Were it not possible for us to see in the history of the past the forces which have issued in the formation of these Religious Societies, we should be inclined to ignore them as agents in the development of the character of the peoples of India. Had Theism no past history we should have to discuss its claims as against those of Christianity by a process of inductive argument, and, granted that the result were that which we have accepted, we should discredit its power over human nature in the present, we should see for it no place in the history of the future, for to us it would seem to be no necessary factor in the Life of Man. But when it can be shown that the Theism of India to-day is the legitimate offspring of the Theism of past ages,[1] modified indeed by new conditions of life, but yet essentially the same, and witnessing to the same essential characteristics of the human heart, we are forced to recognise its claim to a correspondence with the needs of man, we dare not ignore it lest we should be

[1] Hopkins, p. 510. This is not the view of M. Williams, *Theistic Reformers*, p. 11.

shutting our eyes to that Truth which is the only food capable of sustaining human life.

If the Theism of India to-day be the child of the Theism of the past, we must go to the past to understand the present; it is only when we compare the man with his ancestors that we are able to tell whether there be any progress in development or not, whether life be a cycle or a way to an End; and, further, the history of the past tells us that about which the present leaves us in doubt, viz., the result for good or for evil of the emphasizing or neglect of one or other aspect of life; the past has its lessons, its warnings, its encouragements, let the present use to the full the experience gained by the past, the inheritance left by father to son. We shall try to trace in outline the religious genealogies of the Brahmo and Arya Samaj from the earliest times of which we have any record, taking as our test of vital relationship the effort to adhere to the truth of the Unity of God and the consequent unity of man, or to clothe the same truth in warmer language, "the Fatherhood of God and the Brotherhood of Man." We hope to be able by the study of the Present in the light of the Past to answer the question "are the Theistic Reformers of India to-day any nearer to an expression of the truth which will satisfy alike the reason and the affections of men, than were their predecessors? or can this truth be universally accepted and realized in Life only through the acceptance of Historic Christianity?"

THEISM IN INDIA PREVIOUS TO THE BIRTH OF RAMMOHUN ROY.

I. MONOTHEISM IN THE RIG VEDA.

IT is in the Vedas [the books of Indian (Aryan?) wisdom,[1] cf. οἶδα, video, Nor: ved.] the authoritative repositories of the wisdom which the religious ancestors of the Hindu people attained by listening to the voice of Divine Revelation [Sruti,[2] "that which is heard or revealed," is the term applied to literature believed to have been received immediately from the Divine Being] that we first seek for monotheistic teaching. The Vedas, which it is worth our while to remember, were not introduced to the notice of European scholars until the year 1805,[3] by their subject-matter fall under a threefold division: (i) Mantra (man, Latin *mens*, to think), this division consisting of texts, and hymns of prayer and praise; (ii)

[1] Westcott, in *Camb. Comp. to Bible.*.

[2] Williams, *Hinduism*, p. 18.

[3] Barth, p. xxii., note.

Brahmana, the priestly and ritualistic commentaries upon the Mantra; and (iii) Upanishads (*upa-ni-sadin*, sitting below), which are *subsidiary* works of the Ritualistic Brahmanas contained in the Aranyakas or Forest-Books, intended for the use of forest hermits who have passed beyond the need of sacrifice.[1] Their object[2] is the fuller investigation of the abstruse problems suggested by the mysticism of the Brahmanas.

It is with the first of these divisions that we are at present concerned, the second division being devoted to practice rather than thought, and the third belonging to a later period than that into which we would now enquire.

The Mantra portion of the Veda is again sub-divided into four (five) Samhita (collections), viz., the Rig Veda, the Yajur Veda (Black and White), the Sama Veda,[3] and the Atharva Veda. Of these the Rig Veda is the most important, and it is to this that we will confine our enquiry, for the Yajur and Sama Vedas are little more than collections of texts and hymns taken from the Rig Veda and used in the performance of sacrifices, and the Atharva Veda seems in its

[1] Hopkins, pp. 217, 218, 219, footnote. Max Müller, *S. B. E.*, I. lxxix. *sqq.*

[2] M. Williams, *Hinduism*, p. 44.

[3] M. Williams, *Indian Wisdom*, p. 6.

present form to be later than the time of Manu.[1]

The interest and importance of the question before us, whether monotheistic teaching is to be found in the Rig Veda, is enhanced by the appeal to Vedic authority made by the leaders of the Arya Samaj, who by this action have greatly strengthened their position and increased their influence amongst their fellow-countrymen.[2] Yet before citing any passage of the Rig Veda which may be taken as evidence to the existence of a monotheistic creed, attention should be called to the dependence of the meaning of language upon the environment of the speaker or writer. Words that show us the orthodoxy of Origen would from the lips of Athanasius have sounded like heresy. Thought and language alike gain accuracy only through controversy, where in self-defence ambiguity is avoided; and the process of making weapons of offence and defence is no short one. The history of Jewish monotheism shows how slight is the barrier, at an early period of development, between monotheism, polytheism, and

[1] M. Williams, *Indian Wisdom*, pp. 5 and 6. (Contrast Barth, p. 33.) Hopkins, pp. 174-5

[2] *Last Days in England of Rammohun Roy*. Carpenter, pp. 5 and 6; "The Brahmo Samaj," *Encyl. Brit.*, by Sir W. W. Hunter; M. Williams, *Religious Thought and Life in India*. Cap. xx. on Dayananda Sarasvati; cp. also Barth, pp. 154-5 for a similar appeal by various Hindu sects.

pantheism; it may be questioned whether even the prophet Elijah had fully grasped the Unity of God when he bade the people choose between Baal and Jehovah; the people certainly thought that it was only a question of the supremacy of one national God over another, and this after they had listened from childhood to the solemn declaration of the Divine Unity, "the Lord our God, He is One." The title 'Lord of Hosts' affords us an instance of the growth in the meaning of language with the progress of thought; being at first taken to mean that the God of Israel was a God of battle, Who led His people to victory, at a later date it was taken to express the dominion over all created being, over the powers of the hosts of Heaven.[1] Bearing in mind then the limits of language, let us consider the evidence for the existence of monotheistic belief that is offered us in such characteristic passages of the Rig Veda as the following:

RIG VEDA (MANDALA, X. 129).[2]

"In the beginning there was neither nought nor aught,
Then there was neither sky nor atmosphere above.

. . . .

Only the Existent One breathed calmly, self-contained,
Nought else than Him there was—nought else above, beyond."

[1] For the indefiniteness of such terms as 'pantheism,' 'monotheism,' vid. Rhys Davids, *Hibbert Lectures*, p. 21.

[2] M. Williams, *Indian Wisdom*, pp. 19 ff.

RIG VEDA (MANDALA, X. 121).

"What god shall we adore with sacrifice?
Him let us praise, the golden child that rose
In the beginning, who was born the lord—
The *one sole lord* of all that is—who made
The earth and formed the sky, who giveth life,
Who giveth strength, whose bidding gods revere,
Whose hiding-place is immortality."

With such passages as the above we must compare the following which point to a nature-worship closely akin to polytheism through the personification of the distinctive forces of Nature.

RIG VEDA I. 168.[1]

"Self yoked are they come lightly from the sky. The immortals urge themselves with the goad. Dustless, born of power, with shining spears the Maruts (storm-gods) overthrow the strongholds. Who is it, O Maruts, ye that have lightning spears, that impels you within? . . . The streams roar from the tyres, when they send out their cloud voices."

The above citations will suffice as examples of the evidence that may be collected from the Rig Veda to show that the character of its teaching is monotheistic, pantheistic, or polytheistic. It is true that the Rig Veda is a composite work, and represents not one only but many schools[2] of thought; yet the very fact that such opposite opinions should be treasured in the same collection of hymns makes the conclusion that the faith of

[1] Hopkins, pp. 8-11.

[2] *Ibid.*, p. 16.

the many writers of this literature was neither monotheistic, pantheistic, nor polytheistic, but rather a vague[1] and chrematheistic[2] physiolatry, appear to be the most probable. This faith has been called Henotheism, the worship of each divinity in turn as if it were the greatest and even the only god recognised.

"As soon as a new god is evoked, all the rest suffer eclipse before him; he attracts every attribute to himself; he is *the* god; and the notion, at one time monotheistic, at another pantheistic, which is found in the latent state at the basis of every form of polytheism, comes in this way to be ascribed indiscriminately to the different personalities furnished by the myths,"[3] which myths of Nature worship "resolve into physical phenomena."[4] If we accept this view of the religious thought of the Rig Veda, we shall be able to see an orderly development in Hindu theology, from the half-embodied deities to the first immaterial author of the universe, "from the physical beginning of the Rig Vedic religion to its spiritual Brahmanic end";[5]

[1] Hopkins, pp. 135 and footnote (166).

[2] M. Williams, *Indian Wisdom*, pp. 7 and 8; *Encyl. Brit.*, 9th Ed., "Theism." "Henotheism is an imperfect kind of monotheism in which God is thought of as One only because others had not yet presented themselves to the mind, a monotheism of which polytheism is not the contradiction, but the natural development." M. Müller, *Lectures on the Origin of Religion*, pp. 266 and 291-3.

[3] Barth, p. 26. [4] *Ibid.*, p. 178. [5] *Hopkins*, pp. 73, 74.

the Rig Veda, thus interpreted, shows us man seeking for a true conception of God, and not resting satisfied in any one expression of belief. We are conscious that in these days we stand upon a higher level than its writers, viz., that of the "fulness of time" used by God for the enlightenment of man through man: we therefore cannot regard their teaching as final or infallible, though we offer them the reverence due to parents. The monotheist of to-day will welcome their words expressive of belief in the unity of God as a link of truth in the present with truth in the past, and can afford to ignore those sentiments which the light of longer life has shown to be partial or misleading. Theistic reformers may rightly appeal to the Rig Veda for confirmation of their teaching, not as to an all-wise, infallible authority, but as to a child safeguarded by its innocence and lack of bigotry from any wilful perversion of the truth. They will find in it the human heart opened in ready sympathy, eager to learn, eager to worship.

II. Monotheism in the Upanishads.

From the Rig Veda we turn to the literature of a later period to see whether there be in it any trace of a continuous development of religious thought in the direction of a monotheistic belief. Some such development of thought can, we believe, be found in the Upanishads. This literature covers an indefinite period of time.[1] The treatises which bear this name, and have up to the present time been catalogued, number nearly 250.[2] The earlier of these writings, *i.e.* those which occupy a place in the Samhitas, Brahmanas, and Aranyakas, are probably of a date earlier than 600 B.C., and are therefore anterior to the rise of Buddhism.[3] We have already spoken of the meaning of the title Upanishad (p. 12).

With the Upanishads we pass from one class of literature to another; the language of the Rig Veda and the Yajur, Sama, and Atharva Vedas is with some exceptions[4] the unconscious servant of a life full of hopes and fears and of absorbing activity; in the Upanishads, language, as the fruitful mother of thought, rules men's lives in the right of her offspring.[5] Thought is recognised as a power,

[1] Hopkins, p. 216: "In India no literary period subsides with the rise of its eventually 'succeeding' period."

[2] Barth, p. 66.

[3] S. B. E., vol. i., lxvii. Hopkins, pp. 216, 217. For the opposite view see Barth, p. 67.

[4] M. Müller, *Vedanta Philosophy*, p. 144.

[5] Khandogya—Upanishad. 1st Prapâthaka. 13th Khanda, 4.

"Speech yields the milk, which is the milk of speech itself to him who knows this Upanishad of the Samans in this wise. He becomes rich in food and able to eat food."—Dr. Martyn Clark, *Lecture IV.*, p. 8.

II. Aranyaka, 3 Adhyaya and Khanda 4. "Dependent on names they rejoiced in what had been revealed."—M. Müller, *Vedanta Philosophy*, pp. 115, 116, 141.

and speech is identified with thought; hence the importance of such a mystic syllable as Om.[1] Thought is exalted, but not yet as pure thought, because it is yet associated with sound, the abstract with the concrete, motions of the mind with motions of matter. The basis of pantheism is found here, being neither denied by the assumption of antagonism in the form of dualism, nor destroyed by the recognition of the power of self-determination[2] as distinguishing the 'Person' from the 'thing.'

Indian writers distinguish the Upanishads from other Vedic literature by the title 'Jnana Kanda,' 'the department of knowledge,' as distinct from 'Karma-Kanda,' 'the department of works.'[3] Although it be true that "belief in India was never so philosophical that the believer did not dread the lightning,"[4] yet that belief became increasingly philosophical as man by the efforts of his mind became less directly dependent upon the forces

[1] Farrar, *Chapters on Language*, p. 256: "Sound which is the incarnation of thought." Such an identification of thought and sound we believe to be inevitable, and its pantheistic consequences are, we think, also so, unless counteracted by one of the two means (dualism or personification) referred to in the text. See Max Müller, *Science of Language*, vol. ii., pp. 73 ff., "Without speech no reason, without reason no speech."

[2] Kant, *cit.* Illingworth, *Personality—Human and Divine*, pp. 22 and 23. *Tennyson*, *Life of*, vol. i. pp. 311, 312.

[3] M. Williams, *Hinduism*, p. 43. Barth, p. 67. M. Williams, *Indian Wisdom*, p. 33.

[4] Hopkins, p. 37.

of nature. When he learnt that by foresight in the preparation of water-tanks he could make himself comparatively independent of Indra, and await with equanimity the result of the latter's contest with Vritra the cloud-serpent, he began to recognise a power within himself that might, when developed, put him on an equal footing with the objects of his worship.[1] This power was invisible and abstract, and yet often showed itself superior to the visible and concrete. If religion was still to hold its sway, the nature of the gods must be regarded as similar to this greatest power within the experience of man. Thus little by little the religious conception of the divine nature became more abstract, and the moral power of will, or prayer, came to be regarded, under the name Brihaspati, or Brahmaspati,[2] as the Supreme Being. But although the conception of the divine nature becomes even in the Rig Veda thus spiritualised, there is as yet no clear and exclusive personification of moral force. Brihaspati takes the place of Indra,[3] but not to the exclusion of other gods, who representing concrete material force yet hold their place in the pantheon. The writers of the Upanishads, which were intended for the use of those who separated themselves from the world, and have as

[1] Barth, p. 71. [2] *Ibid.*, pp. 15, 16.
[3] Hopkins, 136.

their object the destruction of passion,[1] can afford to ignore that popular conception of the divine nature, drawn from the experience of life, which demands a personal revelation corresponding to the many and various conditions of life, and therefore tends to the multiplication of deities, and can devote themselves to abstract philosophy unhampered by any call to action. To be is their motto, rather than to do. We rise in the Upanishads to a conception of the divine nature as being 'without body, parts, or passions; of infinite power, wisdom and goodness'; but we do this by ignoring factors in the problem of life that is given to man to solve. The belief in one God as opposed to many is of indefinite value until it is made clear whether the unity be one of nature or personality. Such a passage as the following suggests indeed a belief in the unity of person, and the selfish consequences of such a belief are unflinchingly painted by one who has withdrawn himself from the life of the world. "Not for the husband's sake is the husband dear, but for the ego's sake is the husband dear. Not for the wife's sake is the wife dear, but for the ego's sake is the wife dear. . . . Not for the sake of gods are the gods dear, but for the

[1] S. B. E., vol. i., p. lxxxi. M. Müller on the *Origin of Religion*, pp. 324-5; M. Müller, *Vedanta Philosophy*, pp. 15, 18, 22 *sq.*

[Yet this literature is *religious*. See Barth, pp. 77 ff., and Hopkins, pp. 239 f.]

ego's sake are gods dear; not for the sake of anything is anything dear, but for the sake of the ego is anything dear. . . . Where there is as it were duality, there one sees, smells, hears, notices, knows another; but when all the universe has become mere ego, with what should one smell, see, hear, address, notice, know any one else? How can one know him through whom he knows this all, how can he know the knower? The ego is to be described by negations alone, the incomprehensible, imperishable, unattached, unfettered; the ego neither suffers nor fails."[1] The universal ego is identified with the particular ego.[2]

Because these writers did not recognise that human personality can only find full scope through social life, which offers an object for love, and implies a relation between subject and object, they did not feel the need of a "social God, with all the conditions of personal existence internal to himself."[3]

But on the other hand other passages from the Upanishads may be cited which point to the conception of divine unity as being one of nature rather than of person. "Whether the All is personal or impersonal—is still an unsettled point."[4]

[1] Brihad Aranyaka Upanishad, *cit.* Hopkins, pp. 234-5.

[2] Hopkins, 236.

[3] Illingworth, *Personality*, pp. 69-75.

[4] Hopkins, p. 219.

"Whether the immortal impersonal was a being alive and a personal ātmā or whether this personal being was but a transient form of impersonal imperishable being was a point concerning which the sages were in all probability uncertain."[1] In one passage we have presented to us a personal deity, under the Rig Vedic name Prajapati, the father-god; in another passage He is represented as Himself proceeding from a material substratum; in mythic form he is Hiranyagarbha, the golden embryo, who issued from the world-egg.[2]

The belief of the Upanishads is that there is "but one real Being in the universe, which Being also constitutes the universe."[3] This pantheistic creed is spiritualised, the one Being is regarded as spirit; everything material is evanescent, and owes its origin to Maya (illusion) alone.

> "There is one only Being who exists.
> Unmoved, yet moving swifter than the mind:
> Who far outstrips the senses, though as gods
> They strive to reach him; who himself at rest
> Transcends the fleetest flight of other beings;
> Who like the air, supports all vital action.
> He moves yet moves not; He is far yet near:
> He is within this universe, and yet
> Outside this universe: whoe'er beholds

[1] Hopkins, p. 238.

[2] Barth, p. 68; A. E. Gough, in *Encyc. Brit.*, 9th Ed., article "Vedanta."

[3] M. Williams, *Indian Wisdom*, p. 34.

> All living creatures as in Him, and Him
> The universal spirit—as in all,
> Henceforth regards no creature with contempt."[1]

The impersonal character of this spirit is shown by the following: "In the beginning, there was the mere state of being—one only without second. It willed, 'I shall multiply and be born.' It created heat. That heat willed, 'I shall multiply and be born.' It created water."[2] The origin of all things is no more personal than heat or water.

We conclude that in the Upanishads it is possible in the more spiritual conception of God, and the declaration of the essential unity of man with God, to recognise an advance in religious development towards a monotheistic belief; but we do not think that the philosophy here propounded is safeguarded against a pantheistic interpretation. The language of Jean Paul in one of his dreams is descriptive of the religious thought of the Upanishads. In his dream his eye was opened and a sea of light filled all Creation; his heart felt the presence of an unspeakable power, swelling in varied forms of existence around him. Suns and planets were seen to float as mere specks in the ocean of life which was revealed to him. . . . But in this glorious splendour his guide had vanished. He

[1] M. Williams, *Indian Wisdom*, p. 36.
[2] *Ibid.*, p. 39.

was alone in the midst of life.[1] The loneliness of life as exhibited in the Upanishads is glorious, but incompatible with human life: if this be the perfect revelation of God, no man can see His face and live.

III. Connection between later Religions and the growing Monotheism.

Leaving the Upanishads we must in the course of our enquiry as to the antecedents of modern theism touch but very lightly on those religious movements which, while they register a protest against the polytheistic and pantheistic tendencies of the day, do not contribute a monotheistic solution to the problems of life. Thus in the case of Buddhism we have a philosophy presented to us that starts from different premises from those upon which the religions of the world rest. "It can only by courtesy be called a religion at all."[2] "The distinguishing characteristic of Buddhism was that it started on a new line, that it looked at the deepest questions men have to solve from an entirely different standpoint. It swept away from the field of its vision the whole of the great soul

[1] Jean Paul, cited Westcott, *Gospel of Resurrection*, pp. 1 and 2.

[2] Marcus Dods, *Mohammed, Buddha and Christ*, p. 129; Wilson, *Select Works*, vol. ii., p. 361.

theory which had hitherto so completely filled and dominated the minds of the superstitious and of the thoughtful alike. For the first time in the history of the world it proclaimed a salvation which each man could gain for himself—without the least reference to God, or to gods, either great or small."[1] "A system like this, in which our whole well-being—past, present, and to come—depends on ourselves, leaves little room for a personal God."[2] Buddhism is the expression of the pessimistic atheism[3] of the age which produced the Chokmah literature of the Hebrews; these latter, hoping against hope, by an effort of faith sought refuge from pessimism in a theistic creed: "vanity of vanities, saith the preacher; all is vanity." "Let us hear the conclusion of the whole matter: Fear God and keep his commandments"; but Gautama found the solution not in thought but through the glorious inconsistency of his life; preaching pessimism, he by active love inspired his followers to optimism; proclaiming atheism, he offered himself to his disciples in the place of the Deity. His unselfish love removed the barrier of caste, and in him the devotee found refuge. The Buddhist's confession of faith is this, "I take refuge

[1] Rhys Davids, *Hibbert Lectures*, pp. 28, 29.

[2] Sir W. W. Hunter, *Brief History of Indian Peoples*, p. 77.

[3] For a definition of the 'atheism' of Buddhism see Westcott, *Gospel of Life*, pp. 166-7.

in Buddha, in the doctrine, in the Church."[1] We do not then in Buddhism find that direct advance towards monotheism which we believe can be traced in the Rig Veda and in the Upanishads; and yet indirectly it has borne fruit. It reacted upon Brahmanism and led to fresh efforts being made by such men as the 'Revivalist preacher'[2] Sankara-Acharya to set the theology of the day upon a level with the fuller revelation of the Divine in human experience. The immediate result was the formation of the various schools of philosophy, each emphasizing one side of the truth. Of Jainism, even though it arose earlier than Buddhism,[3] we need not speak here, for its distinctive features are imperceptible: it has neither the marked divergence from Brahmanism in its essential principles that gives Buddhism its chief interest, nor does it differ from Buddhism except in the direction of pantheism. The Jains are described as being "of all the sects the most colourless and insipid."[4]

[1] Hopkins, pp. 313-321; M. Dods, pp. 181 ff.; Wilson, *Select Works*, vol. ii., pp. 337-339, 355-357.

[2] M. Williams, *Hinduism*, p. 83, "of whom it has been said that since his short life in the 8th or 9th century everv Hindu sect has had to start with a personal God"; Hunter, *Brief History*, p. 100.

[3] Hopkins, p. 283. For the opposite opinion, *vid.* Barth, p. 146 *sq.*

[4] *Ibid.*, p. 296.

IV. Monotheistic Tendencies in Saivaism and Vaishnavism.

In Saivaism we have the faith of the Brahmans, in Vaishnavism that of the people.[1] In the essential teaching of the former we find traces of monotheistic belief; and we find the same in the reforming sects of the latter. Saivaism represents the Sankhya system of philosophy, the tendency of which is monotheistic, whilst Vaishnavism represents the pantheistic philosophy of the Vedanta.[2] "As soon as Saivaism becomes popular and develops into a religious system for the masses, it at once gives up Siva and takes up Vishnu, or keeping Siva it drops pantheism and becomes a low form of sectarian asceticism. Saivaism is, therefore, fundamentally Unitarian."[3] It would seem that thoughtful men, in the first centuries after the Christian era, whose orthodoxy would not permit them to accept the atheistic doctrines of Gautama, and who yet found no rest in the unphilosophic religion of the Mantra portion of the Vedas, turned to Saivaism as offering them the calm repose that a belief in one Supreme Being can alone afford. Saivaism lost its hold upon such men

[1] *Encycl. Bri.*, 9th Ed., art. "Hindustani," by Charles James Lyall. Wilson, *Select Works*, vol. i., p. 191.

[2] Hopkins, p. 484. [3] *Ibid.*, p. 485.

through the fascination of the Vaishnavite philosophy, presented with new and living power by Sankara-Acharya.[1] Pure Saivaism does not appeal to facts as such; its claim upon men for acceptance rests upon its correspondence to the requirements of man's intellect; hence the more simple monotheistic belief is out-bidden by the pantheistic philosophy which attracts men by the innumerable questions which it raises. The failure of Saivaism to hold its own is due to its want of connection with the facts of life; it does not, in Northern India, offer to its adherents even the semblance of an historic faith; its literature as known in Northern India is without the inspiring epic poem, so great a source of strength to Vaishnavism and Krishnaism; only in the south where it treats local manifestations of Siva as being historical persons does it yet rival Vaishnavism; it succeeds to the extent that it is inconsistent with itself.[2] We find then in the stricter form of Saivaism a theism, not indeed guarded by clear definitions against the charge of being pantheistic,[3] but yet differing from Vaishnavism as monism from pantheism. And this form of Theism appears to fail in its effort to satisfy the needs of men so far as it keeps itself pure by seclusion from the world.

[1] Hopkins, pp. 488-9. [2] Wilson, *Select Works*, vol. i., pp. 188-190.
[3] Hopkins, p. 484, footnote 2.

It claims to speak about, comment upon, interpret the facts of life, but it cannot claim these very facts as the expression of itself.

Our interest in Vaishnavism, on the other hand, centres about its reformers; about those men who could no longer brook the degrading confusion of truth and falsehood, of fact and illusion, of right and wrong, which belongs to pantheism.[1] These men sought freedom by the assertion of their belief in the unity of the Supreme Being. Of these the leading minds were Ramanuja, Madhva, Vallabha, and Chaitanya, and, under direct Mohammedan influence, Kabir and Nanak;[2] we will briefly enquire into the distinctive characteristics of each of these attempts at Theistic reform.

Ramanuja founded his Protestant sect about the middle of the 12th century;[3] this *sampradaya*, or sect, was known as the Sri Sampradaya. Born in Southern India about the end of the 11th century, Ramanuja spent the early years of his life in converting Saivas to Vaishnavism. Even when Saivaism during the reign of Krimi Konda Chola had the support of the throne, Ramanuja refused to conform to its teaching, and had to

[1] For an account of the reformer Swami Narayan, see *Hinduism*, M. Williams, pp. 145-6. Heber, *Indian Journal*, vol. ii., pp. 108 *sq.*

[2] Royal Asiatic Society, M. Williams, *Indian Theistic Reformers*, p. 2.

[3] Wilson, *Select Works*, vol. i., pp. 35 *sq.* Barth, p. 194.

escape for his life to Mysore. This shows him to have been faithful to the Vaishnavite body, although ready himself to differ from his teachers on certain points. In opposition to Vedantic Vaishnavism, Ramanuja and his followers have maintained that the Deity is endowed with all good qualities and with twofold form, the supreme spirit, the cause, and the gross spirit, the effect or matter.[1] So far as the former, the Paramatma, is concerned, we find unity and that distinct from the world, but this supreme spirit finds its complement in the gross spirit which is one with the world, and here lies the foundation of pantheism. The Deity is not in the fulness of his nature, but only in one form, distinct from the world. Hence not Vishnu alone, but also Laksmi and their respective incarnations are objects of worship to the Ramanujas.[2] The conception of an incarnation is clearly that of a "conversion of the Godhead into flesh," not of "the taking of the manhood into God."

Madhva, or Ananda-Tirtha, was born about 1200 A.D.[3] All the Madhavas are Brahmans, for Ananda-Tirtha was a strict observer of caste distinctions.[4] He himself encouraged idolatry, treat-

[1] Wilson, *Select Works*, vol. ii., p. 43. Hopkins, pp. 497 *sq.*

[2] Wilson, *Select Works*, vol. ii., p. 38.

[3] Wilson, p. 139, gives 1121 A.D. as date of his birth.

[4] Barth, p. 196.

ing an image of sacred clay recovered from a submerged vessel as an object for special devotion.[1] The Madhavas identify Vishnu with the Supreme Spirit, as the pre-existent cause of the universe, from which, however, it is essentially distinct; yet this distinction is not that between spirit and matter, but between absolute being and life, between the Supreme Spirit and the principle of life, between the Jívátmá and the Paramátmá.[2] Thus it seems that the Madhavas may be regarded as monotheistic so far as the Deity is to them an abstract conception apart from life, but when they think of the Deity as living their faith tends to become pantheistic; in life spirit and matter are united, though not thereby becoming identically the same.[3] When in all living being is recognized the presence of God, and absolute lifeless Divine Being is the object of enthusiastic devotion, pantheistic idolatry appears to be inevitable. Such pantheism is excluded when the Deity is regarded as a Being independent for His life of the life which surrounds Him, as having life in Himself. Through separating the Supreme Spirit from life, Ananda-Tirtha and his followers have made a pure monotheism untenable, for the God whom they seek is the God of the living, and must therefore be Him-

[1] Wilson, *Select Works*, vol. ii., pp. 140, 141.

[2] *Ibid.*, pp. 143-4.

[3] *Ibid.*, pp. 144-5, footnote 4.

self the source of life; if life be not essentially in Him it must be sought elsewhere, and the faith of the seekers becomes dualistic.

Vallabha, who was born in 1479,[1] proclaimed a doctrine of pure non-dualism (Suddhādvaita). As a consequence of this he taught that to renounce well-being was to insult the Deity,[2] teaching which has been carried by his disciples to excess and made the excuse for licentious indulgence of the grossest kind. The object of adoration amongst the Vallabhas is the infant Krishna, as Bálagopála,[3] who is regarded as one with the universe,[4] which derives its existence from him. He is exempt from Maya (illusion) and all qualities, eternal alone, the supreme soul of the world;[5] yet he himself gave birth to Maya and to all the divine beings—Vishnu, Brahma, Durga, Radha, and others. In this sect we can see but little progress towards monotheism beyond the protest against a theism that separates God from life; Krishna is formally recognized as supreme, but his worshippers are ready to recognize other gods, holding subordinate positions, as yet sharing his nature.

[1] Williams, *Hinduism*, p. 143. [Hopkins, p. 504, regards Vallabha Swami as founder of the sect, 16th cent.; see Wilson, p. 120.]

[2] Barth, p. 234.

[3] The child shepherd.

[4] Wilson, *Select Works*, vol. i., p. 121, footnote 1.

[5] *Ibid.*, pp. 122-3.

We see no distinction drawn between the spiritual and material, divine and human, but between the Maker and the made: the distinction between Krishna and man is not one of nature but of relative position; the former creating man clothes the formless with illusive form, the eternal divine with transitory matter; so far as anything *is* it is divine. Such a doctrine when held by men, who by the conditions of their life are compelled to act upon the assumption that the things they see and feel are real, becomes pantheistic, as they forget to regard their surroundings as illusive (the effect of Maya) they look upon them as divine. This distinction between Maker and made is not sufficient to prevent confusion of thought and worship when the nature of both is regarded as the same. Such a difficulty arises from the assumption of the eternity of matter, if real, or else its illusiveness, on the principle 'out of nothing can nothing be made.[1]

CAITANYA. The sect which takes its name from Caitanya is a yet more lamentable instance than the last of the degradation of a society which claimed to reform that body from which it sprang. Its founder was born in 1485. His nature was emotional to an extreme. His devotion was offered

[1] For the assertion of the contrary principle, see Rufinus in *Symbolum Apostolorum*, cit. Heurtley, p. 132, Omnis creatura ex nihilo est.

to Krishna, and was of a sensuous type, that of ἔρως rather than of ἀγάπη, of natural affection than of disciplined will.[1] It seems probable that he lost his life through drowning in the Jumna when in a state of half-conscious ecstasy.[2] The Caitanyas worship Krishna as the Supreme Spirit and both the cause and substance of creation ; as Creator he is Brahma, as Preserver Vishnu, as Destroyer Siva, and yet only one God. Even as He reveals a distinct face (προσῶπον) under varying circumstances, so also He reveals Himself to man, when occasion demands, as an incarnation (Avartara). The effect, as well as purpose, of such a declaration of monotheism as this, in the face of virtual pantheism, has been to supersede the necessity of self-denial and effort of mind or body. The purpose of man's life will be fulfilled if he devotes himself absolutely, without restraint, in affectionate love (Bhakti) to the person of Krishna, which person may for a time be a human being. We need not dwell upon the obvious dangers attending such a false monotheism as this ; the declaration of the unity of God demands that those who worship Him should do so without reserve, but they who obey this call and yet seek Him in the world, instead of through the world,

[1] Hopkins, pp. 503-4 ; Bhattacharjee, pp. 459-471.

[2] Wilson, *Select Works*, pp. 155-61.

are in a worse position than any polytheist; ignoring the distinction between the good and the evil which is present in this world, they consecrate themselves to any form or being that appeals to them, as though it alone had a claim upon them. A polytheist may at least choose as his favourite deity the pure and the good, and neglect the immoral, but he who sees but one Being manifested alike in pure and filthy forms is bound to lose what sense of moral goodness he ever possessed.

KABIR. In that reforming sect, the rise and tenets of which we now make the subject of our enquiry, we can distinctly trace the influence of Islam. Such an influence can indeed be seen in some of those religious bodies which we have already mentioned, for it is probable that their monotheism was the result of contact with Muhammedanism rather than with Christianity;[1] but in the case of Kabir and his followers we are left no longer in doubt as to such connection with Islam. Kabir himself is said by some to have been born in the Muhammedan faith.[2] Setting aside the legendary account of his life of 300

[1] Hopkins, p. 509; Barth., pp. 211, 212.

[2] *Encyc. Brit.*, article on "Hindustani Literature," by C. T. Lyall; Barth., p. 240.

For the contrary opinion see Wilson, *Select Works*, vol. i., p. 69, note 74.

years upon earth, it is thought that he lived in the early part of the 15th century.[1] He showed great boldness in his attacks upon idolatrous worship, though at the same time he permitted the adoration of various deities as representing one God. His object was to unite Hindus and Muhammedans in a common faith. The Universal Name of the One Being he proclaimed to be "The Inner," whether invoked as Allah by Muhammedans or as Rama by Hindus.[2] Of his followers, such as live in the world conform outwardly to the usages of their tribe and caste, but those who are free from the fetters of social life abstain from all the ordinary practices, and address their homage exclusively to the invisible Kabir.[3] An accepted maxim with them is this: "Associate and mix with all, and take the names of all; say to everyone: 'yes, sir; yes, sir.'"[4]

The One God whom they worship has a body formed of the five elements of matter—he is able to assume any shape he will. He is not essentially different from man. He is eternal even as the matter of which he consists is eternal.

[1] Wilson, *Select Works*, vol. i., pp. 71, 72 *sq.*; Barth., p. 238; Hunter, *Brief History*, p. 104.

[2] M. Williams, *Hinduism*, p. 142; Hunter, *Brief History*, p. 104; Wilson, *Select Works*, vol. i., pp. 7-9 *sq.*

[3] Wilson, *Select Works*, vol. i., p. 75.

[4] *Ibid.*, p. 75, iv.

God and man are in the same manner everything that lives and moves and has its being. The differences between man and man of faith, of hope, and of fear, are due to Maya, illusion, originating with the Divine Being.[1]

As we try to estimate the value of the teaching of Kabir, the hopelessness of making any progress through mere syncretism is forced upon us. The reformer's labour appears fruitless when he breaks down idols, only to become, against his will, himself the object of idolatrous worship. The power of Islam opened the mind of Kabir to the need of recognizing the Unity of God, and he set himself whole-heartedly to do so, greeting Muhammedans as his brothers in the truth; but the conception of unity which he possessed was not that which lent force to Islam,[2] that was a Unity of Person, his was a Unity of Nature. It is true that the belief in God as One Person is sadly defective, and does not correspond to the fulness of life; but it was this narrow creed that, by its simplicity and clear definition, separated Moslems from 'Infidels,' and at least helped to make Muhammedanism a power.[3] The creed of Muhammed has been regarded by some Christians

[1] Wilson, *Select Works*, vol. i., pp. 91-92; *Encycl. Brit.*, article "Hindustani Literature."

[2] Maurice, *Religions of the World*, p. 21.

[3] *Ibid.*, p. 22.

as a necessary stage in the religious development of a nation[1]; by separating God from the world it makes clear the relative position of God above, and man below, of Maker and made; it shows idolatry to be what it is. But Kabir did not accept the principle upon which Islam rests; and although he tried, he tried in vain, to enforce its precepts. He would not relax his hold of that which he was assured was true, that God's relation to man is that of a Father. He tried to enforce Muhammedan precepts upon the basis of Hindu principles, monotheistic teaching upon a pantheistic foundation, and failed. He failed because the solution of the problem in the actual course of history had not been made known to him.

NANAK. Where Kabir failed Nanak, in the eyes of the world, succeeded; he alone of Hindu Reformers founded a national religion.[2] It is important that we should seek the answer to the question: 'Why did the pupil succeed where the teacher failed?' 'Was the success of Nanak due to any essential difference between his system and that of Kabir, or to the different circumstances of the times?' Nanak Shah was born near Lahore at the end of the 15th century. Following in the steps of his predecessor, Kabir, he

[1] Trench, *Mediaeval Church History*, p. 56.

[2] Wilson, *Select Works*, vol. i., p. 69.

attempted to combine Hinduism with Islam, promulgating his doctrines in the *Adi Granth* (First Book), which prohibits idol worship, and teaches the Unity of God pantheistically.[1] This book has become an object of worship.[2] Nanak's teaching differed from that of Kabir in his general acceptance of the principles of Vedantic philosophy, which involve the denial of any quality or form in the Divine Being;[3] his teaching is therefore not so grossly pantheistic as that of the latter; he accounted for phenomena by the Vedantic assumption of Maya, illusion. In its devotional aspect his teaching is beautiful in its recognition of the Fatherhood of God, as is shown in the following lines:

> "Thou art the Lord—to thee be praise;
> All life is with thee.
> Thou art my parents, I am thy child—
> All happiness is derived from thy clemency."

Yet it is not to this recognition of the Fatherhood of God, nor to the principle of bhakti (devotion), which was held in common with other reformers, who based their distinctive teaching on Vedantic philosophy, that we can attribute the power over men of the Sikh religion. Its power

[1] Sir M. Williams, *Indian Wisdom*, p. 325, note.

[2] Wilson, *Select Works*, vol. i., p. 268, vol. ii., p. 141, "they worship the visible type of the Khalsa (national identity, *vid. ibid.*, p. 135) in the book."

[3] *Ibid.*, pp. 269 and 91.

was due to a principle adopted from the creed of the Mussulman, viz., the worship of force as such. Had not his successors advanced upon the creed of Nanak, it is probable that the Sikhs or 'disciples' would never have been known as a nation; but the tenth Guru, or master, Guru Govind, established the worship of the sword. In the weakness of the theology of Nanak we may indeed see that which led to the political strength of the Sikh religion, but this does not alter our estimate of his teaching. Because Nanak failed to offer to his disciples a revelation of God which should make them satisfied in worshipping Him alone, they had recourse to hero-worship, regarding Nanak and his successors as Incarnations of the Divine; in this way individual men came to have supreme power over their countrymen, and a monarchy being thus established on a religious basis, it needed but the fitting occasion to transform it into a military and political power, and this was done by the fifth Guru—Guru Arjun—and yet more markedly by Guru Govind,[1] who "threw open his faith and cause to all castes, to whomsoever chose to abandon the institutes of Hinduism, or belief in the mission of Muhammed, for a fraternity of arms and a life of predatory

[1] Barth., pp. 245-6 (according to Wilson, *Select Works*, vol. ii., p. 127, Arjun was the 4th Guru, after Nanak); Hopkins, p. 511.

daring.[1] The orders issued to his disciples, who now assumed the title Singh (lion), by their religious and military head were these: "If you meet a Muhammedan, kill him; if you meet a Hindu, beat and plunder him."[2] So entirely had the sword become the object of their worship that Govind required every Sikh to wear upon his person some emblem of steel;[3] loyalty to their one leader seems to have taken the place of their consecration to One God, their salutation being, "Hurrah for the Unity of the Guru."[4] Circumstances over which Nanak and his successors had no control did, without doubt, tend to make their creed a national one. Thus the persecution of non-Mussulmans by Aurangzeb, in 1677,[5] united the Hindu sects of Northern India, and turned the Sikhs from quietism to militarism. The disciples of Nanak have made for themselves a name in history, but they have done so not owing to, but in spite of, their religion, not through exalting it, but by destroying it; it is said to-day that "the Sikh religion scarcely deserves the name of a religious faith."[6] Looked upon as a

[1] Wilson, *Select Works*, vol. i., p. 273.

[2] Hopkins, p. 512; Wilson, *Select Works*, vol. ii., p. 143.

[3] Wilson, *Select Works*, vol. ii., pp. 129 and 131.

[4] *Ibid.*, p. 129.

[5] Hunter, *Brief History*, p. 148; also pp. 151-213.

[6] Wilson, *Select Works*, vol. ii., p. 149.

religious movement, that which had Nanak Shah as its leader seems to share in the failure that met the attempts of Kabir at reformation, and for the same reason, viz., its shallow syncretism which ignores fundamental divergencies of belief.

THE RISE OF THE BRAHMO SAMAJ

HAVING followed from the earliest times the various efforts made by the ancestors of the natives of modern India to formulate a pure Theistic Creed, we are now in a position to judge the character, and to some extent the future, of the two Theistic Societies, the Brahmo Samaj and the Arya Samaj.

The Brahmo Samaj owes its origin to the labours of the great and good man Rajah Rammohun Roy, who was born in 1772 and died in England in 1833.[1] His character of patient endurance in the cause of what to him seemed to be the truth was shown even in his earliest years. At the age of sixteen he composed a tract against idolatry. In this pamphlet we see the result of the union in a thoughtful mind of the opposite doctrines of Islam

[1] *S.B.E.*, vol. I., p. lxii., footnote, gives 1774 as the date of his birth, as also does Slater, *The Brahma Samaj*, p. 23. I accept the date given by M. M. Williams, *R.A.S. Journal.* Jan. 1881, p. 4, *Encyc. Brit.*, 9th Ed. article, "The Brahma Samaj."

and Vaishnavism. In his college life at Patna he listened to the greatest Muhammedan teachers, at home he came under the influence of his pious Vaishnavite parents. At school he learned to despise the extravagant stories of the Puranas, at home he learned the need of a kindlier creed than that of Muhammed—no wonder then that he sought even so early in life to unite these opposing creeds in one that should satisfy the demands alike of head and of heart.[1] The publication of his first tract stirred up such a feeling of animosity against him that he had to leave his home; he betook himself first to Benares, where he received instruction in the Vedas from the learned Brahmans, to which caste he himself belonged. From there he went to Thibet that he might learn the tenets of Buddhism from its adherents rather than its opponents; his genuine desire to form a fair judgment of the merits of every creed being further evidenced by his learning the language in which each of these finds its expression: thus he studied Sanskrit that he might rightly understand the Vedas, Pali that he might read the Buddhist Tripitaka, Arabic as the key to the Quran, Hebrew as that to the Old, and Greek as that to the New Testament.

[1] *R.A.S. Journal*, Jan. 1881, p. 4 *sq.*; *S.B.E.*, vol. I., p. lxii.; *M. Carpenter's Life*, pp. 37 *sq.*

At the age of twenty he returned to his home, where the affection of his father, conquering his religious prejudices, gave him a warm welcome. Consideration for his father's feelings acted as a restraint upon him until the latter's death in 1803, Shortly after this his brothers also died, and Rammohun Roy succeeded to their share, as well as his own, in his late father's property. He thus became more free than at any previous time to follow the bent of his own inclinations, and he now spent a considerable sum of money in the free distribution of his various works, notably of his pamphlet, *Against the Idolatry of All Religions*, which was written originally in Persian. Yet the possession of wealth which in one way made him independent, became in another a serious hindrance to his projects, for the tenure of his property depended upon his formal retention of the customs of his caste. This fact had considerable influence upon the character of that movement of which he was leader: Rammohun Roy had constantly to declare that he had no intention of breaking away from the religion of his ancestors, but wished to restore it to its original purity. Accordingly he was not satisfied with publishing criticisms of various forms of idolatry, but undertook the translation into Bengali, Hindustani and English of an abridgment of the Vedanta, and of selected portions of the Veda; of the latter the Upanishads appealed to him more than the earlier Mantra portions, because of their lofty tone and correspondence to his own spiritual yearnings; he did not hesitate, however, even in the publication of these books, to omit portions at his own discretion; his individual judgment was to be the test of worth.[1]

At this period of his life he held office under the British Government as Dewan or managing officer, his early antipathy to the English having been overcome; his character was such that he was highly valued by his employers and was able to make a considerable income by his profession; after ten years spent in this office, during which his attitude towards the idolatry of his fellow-countrymen became increasingly antagonistic, he was able to retire to an estate, which he purchased, in a suburb of Calcutta. This was in the year 1814.[2] At his private house he now gathered a considerable number of Hindu and Jain friends from the neighbouring city and led them by his conversation to recognize the need to restore their faith to its original form, casting aside all contemporaneous or later idolatrous accretions. We notice that the retention of any part of the Sacred Scrip-

[1] *S.B.E.*, vol. I., pp. lxiii. *sq.*; *R.A.S. Journal*, Jan. 1881, pp. 4-5; Slater, pp. 24-26; *R. R.'s Last Days*, pp. 3-8.

[2] *R.A.S. Journal*, *ci. sup.*, pp. 5-7; Slater, p. 24; *R. R.'s Last Days*, p. 4.

tures was to depend not upon its early date but upon its intrinsic value. In 1815 he and his friends resolved to form a society amongst themselves for spiritual improvement; to this body was given the name of "Atmiya Sabha," "Spiritual Society." However, the opposition raised by Brahmans, who were present at some of their discussions, and whose arguments were swept aside by the Reformers, proved too great and this society gradually dissolved. Rammohun Roy was now forced to look more than ever to foreigners for the sympathy and moral support which his countrymen were not yet ready to give him. Doubtless the fact that Christians warmly supported him led him to form the more favourable opinion of the teaching of the Founder of Christianity; in 1820 he published a selection, chiefly from the Synoptic Gospels, of the sayings of Christ, under the title, *The Precepts of Jesus, the Guide to Peace and Happiness.*"[1] Of the character of this work and of the motives which led to its production, we will reserve our judgment until we sum up the teaching of Rammohun Roy as a whole. The immediate result of the publication was a warm controversy between *The Friend of India*[2] and the author; the latter appealed to the

[1] *R.A.S. Journal, cit. sup.*, p. 8; Slater, pp. 25-26; *Last Days*, p. 10.

[2] A publication of the Serampore Christian missionaries.

Christian Public against the charge of anti-Christian teaching. Up to this point the controversy had been carried on under pseudonyms, but on the appearance of this "First Appeal," Dr. Marshman of Serampore College entered the lists against Rammohun Roy, who also now declared his identity, and wrote two answers: the 'Second' and the 'Final' Appeal to the charges made against him. These documents form valuable evidence as to the nature of his teaching.[1]

Amongst the Christians with whom Rammohun Roy came in contact was a Mr. Wm. Adam, one of the Serampore missionaries; this man welcomed the efforts at reform which Rammohun Roy was making, and the latter became for some time a regular attendant at services conducted by him. Little by little Rammohun Roy gained such influence over his friend that Mr. Adam became a Unitarian; this success in inducing a Christian teacher to embrace his own views encouraged Rammohun Roy to start a religious community which should include foreigners as well as his own countrymen amongst its members. His aspirations appear thus to have risen from the mere reform of the Hindu Faith to the establishment of an universal religion. In 1828 this, the seed of the

[1] *R.A.S. Journal, cit. sup.*, pp. 8-11; Slater, pp. 25-26; *Last Days*, pp. 11-16.

Theistic Church of India was sown; in 1830 the buildings of the Society were opened, and a trust-deed drawn up in which the building was set apart for services conducted according to the principles of the Brahma Sabha or Brahmiya Samaj, that is to say "The Assembly or Society of God."[1] It was at the same period of his life that Rammohun Roy attained great success in the direction of social reform, for it was mainly owing to his efforts and more especially to his showing that the practice of Suttee found no sanction in the Vedas, that this abominable custom was made illegal in British India in the year 1829.[2] With the foundation of the Brahmo-Samaj we are brought to the close of this brief sketch of its founder's life; alike in the social and the religious spheres of his labour he had met with marked success, but he felt that this needed to be pushed farther by his visiting England; he hoped by his presence there to prevent the possible repeal of the law against Suttee, and also to enlist the sympathies of Christians in England on behalf of those who were trying to enlighten their fellow-countrymen. At the close of the year 1830 he left India, and after two and a half years spent in the eager

[1] Mozoomdar, p. 231; *R.A.S. Journal, cit. sup.*, pp. 10-11; Slater, pp. 26-27; *Encyc. Brit.*, 9th Ed., article "Brahma Samaj."

[2] Sir M. M. Williams, *Religious Thought and Life in India*, cap. xix.

prosecution of his duties in Europe he died on September 27th, 1833.[1] We are more concerned now with the nature of his work than with the character of the man, and yet the two cannot be separated, his great abilities and the enforced limitations of his early environment have alike left their mark for good and for evil upon the society he founded. Both the writings of the man and the trust-deed of the first meeting-house of the Brahmo-Samaj witness to a noble spirit of liberality, which finds its source in deep love of man as man. The following is an extract from the trust-deed referred to, and is quoted at some length because of its importance. "For the worship and adoration of the eternal, unsearchable, immutable Being, who is the Author and Preserver of the Universe, but not under and by any other name, designation or title, peculiarly used for, and applied to any particular being or beings by any men or set of men whatsoever"; . . . "and that, in conducting the said worship and adoration, no object, animate or inanimate, that has been, or is, or shall hereafter become . . . an object of worship by any men or set of men, shall be reviled or slightingly or contemptuously spoken of, or alluded to, either in preaching, or in the hymns or other mode of worship, that may be

[1] *R.A.S. Journal, cit. sup.*, pp. 13-14; Slater, pp. 28-29.

delivered or used in the said messuage or building. . . ."[1] This declaration at once guards the Theistic worship to which it refers from pantheistic idolatry, and prevents any direct or indirect attack upon opposing creeds. Man is to be won to the truth only by its declaration, not by the denunciation of all that is opposed to it. Pleasing as such an attitude is to our minds, we doubt whether it be that which is best calculated to lead to the promotion of the truth in the world as it is: it is hardly that of a church militant. We may contrast with the language of this trust-deed that used by the Apostle St. Paul in denouncing the idolatrous practices into which he saw a tendency amongst Christians to relapse. "Flee from idolatry" . . . "is that which is offered to idols anything? or is an idol anything? No! but the things that the nations offer, they offer to devils and not to God."[2] We take it that the state of the world is such that man can, as a whole, be brought to the truth only by the contrast between darkness and light, truth and falsehood, being forced upon him; before he can learn to desire enlightenment the horror of the darkness that envelops him must be revealed; many in-

[1] *Encyc. Brit.*, 9th ed., article by Sir W. W. Hunter, "Brahma Samaj."

[2] Ellinwood, pp. 115-219; 1 Cor. x, 14, 19, 20.

dividual men there are, like Rammohun Roy himself, whose moral balance seems from early youth to be on the side of goodness, and such men may find what they need in the revelation of goodness alone; gazing upon this they are raised from grace to grace, from imperfection to a perfect moral beauty[1]; but a religion that claims to be universal must, we think, be aggressive[2] as well as contemplative; even amongst those who have become its adherents there must be many whose temptation to relapse into idolatry needs to be counteracted by the stern denunciation of the evil, as well as by the commendation of the good, and this not only in questions of morals, but also in questions of faith. The writings of Rammohun Roy himself at an earlier period of his life, when he was brought into close contact with idolatry in his own home, bear witness to the need of assuming an aggressive attitude; thus he did not hesitate at that time to denounce idol-worship as "the source of prejudice and superstition, and of the total destruction of moral principle, as countenancing criminal intercourse, suicide, female murder and human sacrifice."[3] As his circumstances changed and he found himself the centre of a circle of

[1] Westcott, *Gospel of the Resurrection*, p. 9.

[2] Westcott, *Epp. of St. John*, p. 264, "Essay on the Church and the World."

[3] *R.A.S. Journal*, *cit. sup.*, p. 7.

friends like-minded with himself, and the possibility of removing such gross scandals as Suttee by such secular means as legislation presented itself to him, we think that he became more optimistic and underrated the moral and spiritual degradation with which he had to do; to this undue optimism, rather than to his "too lively sense of the value of money,"[1] do we attribute the vague and comprehensive liberality of his later years. We should not have entered upon this criticism of the liberality of the Brahmo-Samaj at this period of its history, did we not identify its underlying cause with that which prevented Rammohun Roy from acknowledging the Divinity of Jesus Christ. The optimism of the Indian Reformer may be regarded as due to his failure to estimate the nature of sin and of its results in the world. That greatest of all mysteries,[2] the forgiveness of sins, was to him no mystery at all. His conception of the state of man is illustrated by a conversation he had with a lady on the subject of 'original sin'; being asked whether he believed in it, he replied, "I believe it is a doctrine which in many well-regulated minds has tended to promote humility, the first of Christian virtues; for my own part, I have never

[1] *R.A.S. Journal*, *cit. sup.*, 13.

[2] Westcott, *Historic Faith*, pp. 130 *sq*; Dale, *The Atonement*, pp. 315, 316, 348.

been able to see the evidence of it."[1] As we read his words on the forgiveness of sins we see little essential difference between his doctrine and that of Gautama; both alike held a subjective view, and one which makes them independent for forgiveness of any action on the part of God; forgiveness, they both thought, could come through the suffering of the sinner, either, as Gautama, throughout the ages until sin be 'paid for,' or as Rammohun Roy by the sorrow of repentance even in this life. In support of his views the latter writer quoted passages from the Old and New Testaments in which "the forgiveness of God is said to be obtainable by sincere repentance, as required of sinners by the Redeemer."[2] This argument from the Christian Scriptures will have but little weight with those who, recognizing a progressive revelation in the course of history, do not look to find the whole truth in the pages of the Old Testament,[3] and who set side by side with those texts in the New Testament which speak of repentance as necessary to the obtaining of forgiveness, those many other passages which present Christ to us as the objective means through which we are pardoned, as being Himself the

[1] *R. R.'s Last Days*, p. 112. [2] *Ibid*, p. 13.

[3] Not that we can ignore the O.T. teaching of the need of an objective propitiation inculcated by the typical sacrifices.

propitiation for our sins. The thought that was ever uppermost in the mind of Rammohun Roy was the improvement morally, and in every other way, of the human race; it was their 'improvement' rather than their 'salvation.'[1] It is natural that a man's estimation of the character of his deliverer should correspond to his sense of the danger from which he is delivered; it is only when man has abandoned all hope of gaining forgiveness through human effort, that he can recognize Him as Divine Who has power on earth to forgive sins.[2]

In one direction the reforming work of Rammohun Roy will be of permanent value; we think that he turned into a right channel that tendency towards united action which had been debased into a hard and fast system of caste. Each caste is, in the first place, a trade guild. Its members support one another in the event of a trade dispute, and combine to prevent the employment of those who do not belong to their body.[3] In caste, exclusiveness is the correlative of brotherly union. Now other reformers before Rammohun Roy had protested against this narrow exclusiveness, but

[1] Trench, *Hulsean Lectures*, 1846, p. 207, "It was not seen how man had ceased to be a Son of God."

[2] Dale, *The Atonement*, pp. 315-6, 338.

[3] Hunter, *Brief History*, pp. 27, 28; M. Williams, *Hinduism*, pp. 153-4.

the results of their protests were either that caste was ignored only at the moment of intense religious excitement, and resumed its sway as soon as the worshippers returned to their ordinary occupations, or else that a series of new castes took the place of the old.

The reason of their failure to destroy the power for evil, that the system of castes possesses, was this, that its power for good was not utilized by those who would abolish it. The need of common action, of a brotherhood realized in life, was felt so intensely that efforts of a merely negative character to do away with caste met, and we may say met happily, with no lasting response. What was needed, and is needed still, was the full recognition of the principle of brotherhood, not in worship only but also in daily life, and this brotherhood must be shown to include all human beings; such a brotherhood can only be realized through having as its centre one who is unfettered by the bonds of society or even of nationality, one who is indeed the Son of Man; so far as Rammohun Roy led men to Christ as "The Guide to Peace and Happiness" he formed them into an all-inclusive Universal Brotherhood.[1] He is said to have been the first to introduce public

[1] Cambridge Mission to Delhi. *Occasional Paper*, No. 15, Bp. of Lahore.

worship and united prayer amongst Hindus.[1] He may not himself have recognized in full the power of the Name of Jesus, but he did to some degree see in Him the "Way" to God, and preaching God revealed through Jesus, he gave to men as the attractive object of their united worship One Who is all things to all men, regardless of birth or attainments.

It remains for us to consider the attitude adopted by Rammohun Roy towards the Sacred Scriptures, the Vedas, and the Bible. The Vedas he defended against the charge of inculcating idolatry on the ground that, though tolerating it as a last provision for those who are otherwise incapable of contemplating the invisible God of Nature, they repeatedly urge the relinquishment of the rites of idol-worship.[2] It does not seem to have occurred to him to defend one part at the cost of any other, claiming as a reason for doing so the composite character of these books. Yet he did not hesitate to make himself and other men the final judges as to what parts of the Vedas, Quran, Zand-Avasta and Bible are to be accepted as the truth of God. 'The only test of the validity of any doctrine was its conformity to the natural and healthy working

[1] *R.A.S. Journal, cit. sup.*, p. 12; Mozoomdar, p. 24; *Brahmo Year Book for 1879*, p. 27.

[2] *R.A.S. Journal, cit. sup.*, p. 6.

of man's reason, and the intuitions and cravings of the human heart.'[1] We may contrast this attitude of Rammohun Roy with that of Tertullian, who in questions of faith recognized the value of historic tradition for the right interpretation of Scripture.[2] The former seems to us to ignore one of the most important means of arriving at the truth, when he regards himself and his contemporaries as being in an equally favourable position to form an opinion with those who possess a system of interpretation handed down from the time that the writings came into existence. It is only natural that Rammohun Roy should have ignored this factor in the formation of a sound judgment when in the case of the Vedas the commentaries were obviously of a far later date than the texts to which they were appended, and when, in the case of the Old Testament writings, mystic interpretation had taken the place of a once historic tradition; yet none the less did he suffer loss through discarding tradition as a key to the interpretation of the New Testament writings, which has been

[1] *R.A.S.J.*, *cit. sup.*, p. 10.

[2] Tertullian: *de haeret*, § 6, Nobis vero nihil ex nostro arbitrio inducere licet, sed nec eligere quod aliquis de arbitrio suo induxerit. Apostolos Domini habemus auctores, qui nec ipsi quidquam ex suo arbitrio, quod inducerent, elegerunt: sed acceptam a Christo disciplinam fideliter nationibus assignaverunt, § 37, Constat . . . non esse admittendos hereticos ad ineundam de Scripturis provocationem, quos sine Scripturis probamus ad Scripturas non pertinere.

securely kept through the unbroken succession of the historic Church. We must bear in mind when we consider his publication *The Precepts of Jesus*, that he treated the New Testament scriptures apart from their historic setting, even as though they had been written in his own day. It is this that accounts for his extravagant censorship, by which he excluded every fact of our Lord's life which he thought would not commend itself as true to the minds of his readers. Thus he excluded the accounts of Christ's miracles except where they were inextricably interwoven with His sayings, although he himself professed to believe the crowning miracle of the Resurrection.[1]

Since he had approached the Truth through tearing himself away from old associations, it is not to be wondered at that he maintained that it is necessary to right thought to be independent of the thought of others; thus he says that the duty of parents is not so much to impart to their children their own belief, as to prepare their minds in a general way to accept a belief when they are capable of investigating the Scriptures and of listening to arguments from different points of view.[2] We, who as men acknowledge the great debt we incurred when as children we listened to the teach-

[1] Carpenter, *Last Days*, p. 137.

[2] *R.R.'s Final Appeal*, pp. 355-356.

ing which was part of our inheritance, cannot deny a share in this blessing to others; we think that even "the individual believer whose conviction seems and is most independent, would not in reality have been able to attain to it independently."[1] Rammohun Roy appears to have assumed that on attaining a certain age individuals, trained as he would have them without "dogmatic" teaching, would be capable of forming a judgment uninfluenced by other evidence than that then placed before them; the question becomes once more a question of the present state of human nature.[2]

Rammohun Roy, as stated above, defended his publication *The Precepts of Jesus* in three successive "Appeals" to the Christian public. The strength of these is mainly negative, and is due to the attitude assumed by his opponent, who held, according to Rammohun Roy, that the Incarnation was the result of the sins of the world;[3] O felix culpa! a doctrine of more than doubtful historic catholicity. Thus, too, the attacks made by Rammohun Roy upon Trinitarian teaching appear to be due to a misconception of the teaching of the Catholic Church; otherwise we can hardly account for such

[1] V. H. Stanton, *Place of Authority*, p. 74.

[2] For a just appreciation of the value and limits of dogma, see *Life of Tennyson*, vol. i., pp. 310, 311.

[3] See Second and Final Appeal generally, and especially the Final Appeal, p. 415.

words as these: "Early impressions alone can induce a Christian to believe that three are one and one is three; just as by the same means a Hindoo is made to believe that millions are one, and one is millions." The placing by Christian theologians of the Trinity within the Divine *Nature* is here ignored; Rammohun Roy started with the assumption, other than Christian, of the absolute simplicity of the divine nature; and on this assumption he mocked at the conclusions which were not drawn from it; the absolute simplicity of the divine nature is in truth not compatible with the "Christian Trinity of three eternal aspects of the divine nature, facing inward on each other as well as outward on the world,"[1] but neither do we Christians claim such simplicity of nature in the Object of our faith; seen from afar in Old Testament times, the Nature of God was thought to be simple, but as He revealed Himself to men through Christ they saw in Him an ever active Love eternally directed towards an Eternal Object.[2] When we maintain the Unity of the Divine Nature, and the Three Persons within that complex Nature as necessary to its self-satisfying fulness, we cannot think that these words of Rammohun Roy are true: "What-

[1] H. M. Gwatkin, *The Arian Controversy*, pp. 13-14.

[2] Gore, *Creed of the Christian*, pp. 20-23.

Westcott, *Epp. S. John*, pp. 166-219. "The unity is not numerical but essential."

ever argument can be adduced against a plurality of gods strikes with equal force against the doctrine of a plurality of persons in the Godhead; and on the other hand, whatever excuse may be pleaded in favour of a plurality of persons of the Deity, can be offered with equal propriety in defence of polytheism."[1] We will take but one argument against polytheism; "such a system is evil because it leaves its adherents divided between the worship of good and evil, of pure and filthy gods"; can we say this of the Three Persons in the Blessed Trinity? No! because their nature is one, all alike are Holy.[2]

Lastly, what estimate may we form of the value of the Brahmo-Samaj at the time of its founder's death? We think that it was an advance upon the earlier Theistic Reforms, upon that of Ramanuja in its recognition of the independence of the Supreme Being, in the fulness of His nature, of the created world (*vide* p. 31); upon that of Anand-a-Tirtha through breaking with the subtle distinction between Being and Life which led to dualism (*vide* p. 33); upon that of Vallabha by its denial of the sovereignty of evil over man,[3]

[1] *R.A.S. Journal*, p. 9, citation from Final Appeal.

[2] Robson, *Hinduism and Christianity*, p. 247, 'Christianity makes holiness an essential in God. Hinduism makes it an accident.'

[3] It seems very probable that Rammohun Roy's shallow conception of sin was due to a tacit assumption of its derivation from Maya.

(*vide* p. 34) made practical through the acceptance of the sinless man as a guide, instead of the Infant Krishna as an object of worship. The Brahmo-Samaj saved its members from the potentially degrading worship of the divine in man, which characterized the followers of Caitanya, by its express denial of the doctrine of Incarnations; so too, its doctrine of a Unity of Person made the worship of its founder, even after his death (*vide* p. 38), an impious act; it never rested for its power upon the sword, as did the Sikh faith, but spoke with authority through its identification with Western civilization. In short, the Brahmo-Samaj up to this date had avoided the pitfalls that had proved fatal to other efforts at reform, and we cannot value too highly its protest against idolatry, the caste system, and degradation of women, but on the other hand it had given no satisfactory answer to the real problems of life; these problems in later years demanded solution, and the effort to answer them led to schism after schism in the Body. No final answer could it offer because the voice of history was silenced through the undue exaltation of the 'inner-consciousness' of the individual man; thought rather than experience was made the criterion of the truth; in the sphere of thought all may at least claim to be equal; they cannot do so in that of experience. Experience as such was put out of court, and Christianity was treated as a system of philosophy rather than as a revelation of God through facts of history, concerning which some could authoritatively teach others. The answer which history gives to the problems of life was not accepted because the Brahmo Samaj thought before it listened, instead of listening before it thought; it preferred to treat the facts of Christianity as a superstructure upon faith rather than as its foundation.

THE BRAHMO SAMAJ. 1833-1858.

WE return once more to our sketch of the historical development of the Brahmo Samaj. The death of Rammohun Roy was a severe blow to the society; its president, Pandit Ramchandra Vidyavagisa, supported by the late Rajah's friend Dvàraka Nath Tagore laboured earnestly on its behalf, yet it was not until the year 1841, when the latter's son, Debendra Nath Tagore, became its leader that the Brahmo Samaj found a really efficient head.[1] The conditions under which this man was brought up had great influence upon his character and that of the society. Born in 1818 in a home where gross idolatry was practised, he was educated at a Hindu college on principles of avowedly rationalistic philosophy; he sought to base his faith upon reason rather than upon facts interpreted by reason, and took as his spiritual and intellectual guides such writers as Hume and

[1] Slater, p. 33 *R.A.S. Journal*, *cit. supra*, pp. 15-16; Monier Williams, *Religious Thought and Life in India*, p. 20.

Kant; but with manhood he awoke to the need of more deeply spiritual teaching, and with this in view he studied the Upanishads and found in their mysticism that which satisfied him more fully than did the simple precepts of Jesus.[1] At the age of 22 he founded a society for the promotion of the study of the Hindu Scriptures, to which he gave the name Tattvabodhini Sabha, or "The Truth-knowing Society." Two years later Debendra Nath Tagore formally joined the society founded by Rammohun Roy: on his becoming a member of this body he was impressed by its evident need of a properly appointed president, a regularly ordained minister, a settled form of worship, and a fixed standard of faith and practice. At the close of the year 1843 he succeeded in organizing the society, summing up its teaching in definite formulæ, to which its members formally assented, and recognizing Pandit Vidya-bag-ish as the duly appointed minister.[2] The 'Brahmo covenant,' or the vows to be taken by all members of the society, consisted of seven declarations; according to these idolatry was to be abandoned, God, Creator, Preserver, Destroyer, Without Form, was to be worshipped, holy lives were to be led, and forgiveness of sins was to be won through the abandonment

[1] Slater, pp. 32 and 33.

[2] *Keshab Chunder Sen in England*, vol. ii., p. 151.

of sin.[1] This last clause shows us that Debendra Nath's conception of sin was not different from that of Rammohun Roy. During this time the Tattvabodhini Sabha to which Debendra Nath Tagore still belonged issued a monthly journal entitled the *Tattvabodhini Patrika*; the editor of this paper held very liberal views with regard to the infallibility of the Vedic writings; he exercised a great influence upon Debendra Nath and eventually converted him to his own views on the subject of inspiration. The year 1844 may be regarded as that which witnessed the establishment of the first organized Theistic Church of India, at this period known as the Brahmo Samaj of Calcutta. Three years later the number of members had increased to seven hundred and sixty-seven. But throughout this period the rationalistic tendency of his earlier education, supported by the above-mentioned influence of Akhai Kuma Datta, was at work within the mind of Debendra Nath, and was leading to a closer approximation of his doctrine to that of Rammohun Roy in the acceptance of private judgment as the arbiter between falsehood and truth. It was not, however, until the Rig, the Yayur, the Sama, and Atharva Vedas had been carefully studied from this new point of view that their authority as Divinely inspired

[1] *R.A.S. Journal*, *cit. sup.*, pp. 15-17; Slater, p. 34-35.

Scriptures was discarded; this happened in the year 1850. Two years later Debendra Nath issued a revision of the seven declarations and asserted the following four principles: (1) In the beginning was the One Supreme alone, He made the universe. (2) He is eternal, intelligent, infinite, blissful, self-dependent, formless, one only without a second, all-pervading, all-governing, all-sheltering, all-knowing, all-powerful, unmoveable, perfect, and without parallel. (3) By worship of Him alone can happiness be secured in this world and the next. (4) Love towards Him, and performing the works He loves, constitute His worship.[1] With regard to these principles we would call attention to the avoidance of the axiom of the Sankhya philosophy that "out of nothing can nothing be made."[2] We shall see that at a later date God was declared to have created all objects out of nothing.[3] By assuming Creation out of nothing, it became possible to believe in the real existence of created things without their being regarded as part of God; He neither made them out of His own Nature[4] nor

[1] M. Williams, *Religious Thought and Life in India*, cap. xx.; Slater, pp. 35-37; *R.A.S. Journal*, *cit. sup.*, pp. 17-20; *Encyc. Brit.*, article "Brahmo Samaj," Sir W. W. Hunter.

[2] M. Williams, *Hinduism*, appendix, p. 193.

[3] *R.A.S. Journal*, *cit. sup.*, p. 26.

[4] *Vid.* Rufinus in *Symbolum Apostolorum*, Heurtley, pp. 132-133,

was their existence due only to illusion (Maya, cf. above, p. 34); the thought that everything is made out of the thought or will of God and is therefore part of Himself, though essentially true, seems to have been definitely and perhaps wisely laid aside by the Brahmo Samaj, as a dangerous subtlety conducive to pantheism.

The second main principle raises in our minds the question, "How can God be 'all-sheltering,' 'all-knowing,' and 'perfect,' without an Eternal Object of His eternal Love? Is this faith intelligible? can it be thought out?" As we reason from human personality concerning the nature of perfect divine personality, we think that the tri-unity which we find in man of subject, relation and object must be eternally actualized within the Godhead.[1] Further, it is doubtful whether the doctrine of the personality of God was regarded by the Samaj as of great importance; those who desired a more formal initiation into the system, and to be made members of the 'inner church' had indeed to assert their belief in a Personal God, but the essential creed of the congregation was so drawn up as to enable any deist to subscribe to it, the unity being that of impersonal

where the unique character of Christ as the 'Unicus Filius' is supported by an "a fortiori" argument based on this assumption. Westcott, *Epp. S. John*, pp. 218-220.

[1] Illingworth, *Personality*, p. 74.

Nature.[1] Throughout this period the Brahmo Samaj of Calcutta, although it had struck at the very root of the traditional beliefs of India, neither claimed to follow Christ, nor departed from national customs;[2] but a period of change was now at hand, of change made inevitable by the comprehensive character of the Samaj; as fresh members were admitted they made the Society increasingly representative of human nature as a whole, and the craving of the human heart for freedom and for religious warmth, which in the case of the early members of the Samaj had been checked by timid conservatism and intellectual antagonism was bound sooner or later to find expression. We cannot but think that the new movement within the Samaj, of which we are about to give an account, though resting upon insufficient foundation, did nevertheless bear witness to an essential truth; and we think that the very fact that such a movement should have taken place is evidence of the insufficiency of the Brahmo Samaj of Calcutta to satisfy the needs of men. This new movement centres about one individual, Keshab Chunder Sen,[3] but remarkable as this man was for ability, we cannot regard the movement of which he was leader as originating

[1] Hopkins, pp. 516-518, with footnotes; important restrictions upon Sir M. M. Williams.

[2] Mozoomdar, p. 234.

[3] *R.A.S. Journal*, *cit. sup.*, pp. 20 *sq.*

with himself, for even though he had never lived some such movement would, we think, have occurred, and would have found another head; it was the result of "sheer psychological necessity";[1] yet no doubt the striking character of its leader left its stamp upon the new society, and it is well that we should pass in review the personal history and character of this able man. Keshab Chunder Sen was born in the year 1838; his family were zealous worshippers of Vishnu, and in his early childhood he felt the power of enthusiastic devotional fervour. He was educated at the Presidency College, Calcutta, and his intellectual training here proved fatal, for the time, to his faith. But the desire for spiritual exercise yet burnt strongly within him, and little by little he found rest and satisfaction in the revelation to his soul of the Supreme Spirit, and the apparent antagonism between reason and faith ceased to trouble him; within his own soul he found perfect harmony between them, and he cared no longer about the discrepancies which troubled those who did not share his spiritual experiences; he sought no longer to verify the facts of revelation by strict historical research, finding sufficient evidence for them within his own heart. We shall notice presently the consequent subjective character of the new Samaj.

[1] Mozoomdar, p. 203.

At the time when Keshab Chunder Sen was passing through "the crisis of faith," and had already caught glimpses of the life beyond, he came across a tract published by the Brahmo Samaj of Calcutta, which showed him that the views accepted by that society closely coincided with his own, and he accordingly became a member of it; this happened in the year 1858. In the same year Debendra Nath returned from his voluntary exile in the Himalayas, where for three years he had occupied himself in meditation and prayer; his return was marked by a development of the devotional side of the life of the Samaj,[1] and thus rendered it the more acceptable to Keshab Chunder Sen. Between the latter and Debendra Nath there sprang up a warm friendship, and the enthusiasm of the younger man affected his companion, who ventured in the year 1861 to celebrate the marriage of his daughter according to a reformed theistic ritual; yet beyond this point Debendra Nath would not go, and when Keshab pressed the complete abolition of all caste restrictions Debendra Nath refused his consent, and retired once more to the hills. The result was a complete severance between the followers of Keshab who termed themselves "Progressives," and in November 1866 were organized as a New Society under the title the "Brahmo Samaj of India," and

[1] Mozoomdar, pp. 192-3-4.

the adherents of Debendra Nath, who were now known as the Adi Brahmo Samaj.[1]

Having reached the parting of the ways, it may be well to look back upon the past history of the Adi Brahmo Samaj, and to try to estimate its future value as a religious force, before proceeding to sketch the history of the new Samaj.

Owing its origin to the efforts of Rammohun Roy, the (Adi) Brahmo Samaj received its definite organization from Debendra Nath Tagore. During his presidency the fundamental principles of the Society were affected by the decision of 1850, which rejected the doctrine of the infallible inspiration of the Vedas. Although the conservative minority within the Brahmo Samaj did not on this occasion succeed in retaining the principles of Rammohun Roy, these were revived by Dayananda Sarasvati, the founder of the Arya Samaj, and will come before our notice at a later period. Between 1850 and 1858, at which latter date the Bhakti movement began which led to the schism of 1866, the spiritual character, which the personal influence of its founder had imparted to the Brahmo Samaj of Calcutta, seemed to be lost, and its proceedings became mechanical; even such a question as the character of the supreme Spirit being decided by

[1] Mozoomdar, pp. 195-7, 238-9; Slater, pp. 42 *sq.*; *R.A.S. Journal*, *cit. sup.*, pp. 22-26; Hopkins, pp. 518-519

a show of hands.[1] When we try to estimate the value of the Adi Brahmo Samaj, we must recognize to how great an extent its success has been due to the circumstances of the times rather than to its own intrinsic force. Thus its rise has corresponded to the breaking down by European influences of the religions of India; [2] as the effect of Western upon Eastern thought has at first been negative rather than constructive, so too in matters of faith has been the teaching of the Adi Brahmo Samaj; it has been moving with the stream; on the other hand, in questions of practice, it has been conservative, it has escaped opposition by its principle of non-interference with those customs which the natives of India are not yet prepared to give up; its policy has throughout been cautious, because intellectual rather than emotional, for emotional fervour does not stay to look at difficulties.[3] It has followed the path of Western civilization, and because it has not hitherto borne the brunt of the battle we can neither congratulate it upon its victories nor lament any great failure. Our estimate of the value of the Adi Brahmo Samaj must depend upon the value that we attach to the principles of Bhakti, upon

[1] Mozoomdar, p. 192.

[2] Lyall, *Asiatic Studies*, 1st series, pp. 28-29.

[3] Merivale, *Conversion of the Northern Nations*, p. 5.

the place that we assign to emotion in the spiritual life; to those who regard Bhakti with contempt as mere 'hysterical fervour'[1] the negative character of the Adi Brahmo Samaj will appear to be its strength and greatest recommendation[2]; but to those who see in Bhakti an essential element of true religion, the absence of such emotionalism from the fundamental teaching of this Samaj will be sufficient prediction of its future failure to establish itself as an universal church; to them it will not seem "strong enough to exercise an influence with effect on 200,000,000 of men,"[3] to them it will seem to be unable wholly to 'shake off the lingering influence of the old Vedantic Pantheism.'[4]

[1] Hopkins, p. 519. [2] Hopkins, p. 517. [3] Barth, p. 294.

[4] *R.A.S.*, *cit. sup.*, p. 40, p. 26; Tennyson, *Life*, vol. i., p. 67, "The lips of little children preach against you, you that do profess to teach And teach us nothing, feeding not the heart."

THE BRAHMO SAMAJ OF INDIA.

We may now turn our attention more fully to the Brahmo Samaj of India during the period of its existence from the year 1866 down to the present day. Of the creed of the Brahmo Samaj of India at the time of its inauguration the following are the essential points:

(i.) God is the First Cause of the universe. By His will He created all things out of nothing and continually upholds them.

(ii.) The true Scriptures are two, the volume of nature, and the natural ideas implanted in the mind.

(iii.) God Himself never becomes man by putting on a human body. His divinity dwells in every man, and is displayed more vividly in some. Moses, Jesus Christ, Muhammed, Nanak, Chaitanya, and other great teachers appeared at special times and conferred vast benefits upon the world.

(iv.) The Brahmo religion is distinct from all other systems of religion; yet it is the essence of all. It is not hostile to other creeds. What is true in them it accepts. It is based on the constitution of man, and is, therefore, eternal and universal.

(v.) Every sinner must suffer the consequences of his own sins sooner or later in this world or the next. Man must labour after holiness by the worship of God, by subjugation of the passions, by repentance, by the study of nature and of good books, by good company, and by solitary contemplation. These will lead through the action of God's grace to salvation.[1]

Let us consider these articles of faith, comparing them with those of the Adi Brahmo Samaj and with those of the Christian Church. With regard to the first of these articles we have above (p. 69) called attention to the departure by modern theistic reformers from the Sankhyan maxim, 'out of nothing can nothing be made,' which maxim had been the cause of the failure of earlier attempts at reform; we see a step forward in the bold assertion in the creed of the Brahmo Samaj of India of creation out of nothing. Belief in God

[1] *R.A.S. Journal, cit. supra*, pp. 26-27.

as Preserver, itself no new belief, we see asserted in a Theistic as opposed to a Deistic form, "He continually upholds them." God after creation has continued his activity in relation to the world.

The second article is one of great importance as defining revelation. Two sources of knowledge of God are recognized, viz., the book of nature, and the human conscience; do these two sources correspond to the twofold methods of revelation recognized by Christians, the external and objective on the one hand, and the internal and subjective on the other? The question can only be answered by reference to the teaching of the recognized leaders of the Samaj. The conclusion to which we come after studying the writings and lectures of Keshab Chunder Sen and those of his able coadjutor, Pertab Chunder Mozoomdar, is this, that when they speak of the presence of God, and revelation of God in Nature, they think of the universal Divine Immanence in all Being, and of a passive rather than an active self-revelation; in other words, that God's workings in Nature, in the material world, are patent to those, who, listening to the voice of conscience, have learnt to recognize their Maker, but that they do not themselves in the first place awaken man's conscience. Thus subjective thought about God, does, we think, in their teaching, precede objective self-revelation upon

His part. Those who are spiritually enlightened can trace in history the finger of God, but our knowledge of God does not rest upon the knowledge of facts of history. The silence in the writings of these two men on the suoject of the evidence of history concerning God is very striking, and illustrates at once the subjectivity of their faith and its utter contrast with the historic creed of the Christian.

The value to members of the Brahmo Samaj of India of historic records consists not of the facts thus preserved, but of the contemporary interpretation of those facts; they see in such records 'a grand depository of truth attained by the religious consciousness of all nations, under varying modes and orders of development.'[1]

The true character of the teaching of the Brahmo Samaj is somewhat veiled through its emphasizing the thought that the voice within men, which speaks of God, is really His voice and does not originate with themselves. "The religion of the Brahmo Samaj is called a *Dispensation* because the Brahmos have not *made* their religion; it was dispensed to them by One who at once can understand human wants, and satisfy them from the fulness of His mercy and truth;[2] "Inspiration with us is an *objective* reality,

[1] Mozoomdar, p. 77.

[2] Mozoomdar, p. 352.

and as such it is under no necessity to be distinguished as 'ordinary' or 'extraordinary.' All impulses which are objectively perceived to come from God are inspiration with us."[1]

They thus in theory give an objective tone to their creed, but it is in theory only, for as soon as we come to the actual question of the acceptance or rejection of any proposition, it is referred to the judgment of the individual rather than to the judgment of God as revealed objectively and externally. The matter is one of so great importance that we proceed to illustrate the conclusions stated above by quotations from the writings of this Samaj. The following are words of Keshab Chunder Sen when speaking in behalf of the Brahmo Samaj of India in 1872: "As touching the question asked, 'Is Christ our guide?' I revere Christ as a Teacher; to Chaitanya and other Indian prophets too, and to the ancient scriptures of the Hindoos, we are profoundly thankful for our spiritual growth. But we look upon none of these as our guide in the path of salvation. I put it to you, my friends, whether it is Christ that leads me to God, or God who leads me to Christ? Assuredly, it is God who, in the first instance, turns the heart of man and also guides him to such places and persons as

[1] *Brahmo Year Book for* 1880, p. 101.

may help to satisfy his thirst."[1] An examination paper, set in 1873, in Keshab's Brahmo Theological School contained this among its questions, "Prove the absurdity of the assertion that the knowledge of the Divine attributes is derived from scripture or prophet."[2]

Pertab Chunder Mozoomdar appears to define what the Brahmo Samaj of India means by the 'Volume of Nature' and the 'Ideas implanted in the mind,' when in lectures delivered in 1875 he distinguishes Theism from Deism. Of the former he says, "Theism [consists of] two great parts. One of these is what is termed Natural Religion. This is the faith that is formed in man's mind by the action of natural phenomena and laws upon its faculties and instincts. The conceptions and principles of this kind of Theism are, to a certain extent, changeable, inasmuch as men's ideas on natural facts and laws are subject to change. . . . This Theism is man seeking God." "The second part is revealed Theism, the deep spiritual religion produced by the action of God's Spirit within man's soul. [This] Theism is God seeking man."[3] Apparently, so far as things outside us are concerned, we are only enquirers and not the recipients

[1] *The Brahmo Year Book for* 1876, pp. 6 and 7 *sq.*, also Mozoomdar, p. 372. "To us it is not the prophet who reveals God, but God who reveals the prophet."

[2] *Ibid.* for 1877, p. 20.

[3] *Brahmo Year Book for* 1877, p. 21.

through external facts, of Divine Revelation; between Natural Religion and the inward communing of the soul with God there seems in the Brahmo scheme to be no room for 'Revealed Religion'; there is no 'authoritative publication of Natural Religion.'[1]

It is in its fundamental subjectivity that we find the weak point in the teaching of the Brahmo Samaj. It is this that has encouraged its leaders to despise what is generally known as 'Christian Evidences,' to deny the Divinity of Christ, and to lose all sense of proportion in vague spiritualistic mysticism. Thus Keshab made it his boast that he never 'betook himself to the voluminous books which treat of the Evidences of Christianity';[2] because he did not see in history an unveiling of God's purpose independently of his own powers of interpretation he failed to see, in the unique position of Christ in history, evidence of His unique character; Christ was to him a spirit rather than a living man, a spirit who identified Himself with his own spirit; "I . . . draw a line of demarcation between the visible and outward Christ and the invisible and inward Christ, between bodily Christ and spiritual Christ, between the Christ of images and pictures and the Christ that grows in

[1] Butler's *Analogy*, part II., chap i.

[2] *K.C.S. in England*, vol. i., p. 167.

the heart, between dead Christ and living Christ."[1] This last passage will prepare us for the later development of this movement, when Keshab Chunder Sen claimed his independence of all guidance other than the voice of the spirit within him. The following passages from the writings of Pertab will show that his faith was like that of Keshab, intuitional and subjective. "No theology," he says, "have we got, all our theology is our earnest, intense faith in the presence of the spirit of God within us."[2] Whilst questioning the assertion that the Brahmo faith rests on intuition alone, he says, "The germs only, and the germs not merely of the religion of the Brahmo Samaj, but of Christianity, Hinduism, and Mohamedanism alike, are intuitions; the peculiarity of the Brahmos being that they build their faith thereon without the supernatural and historical groundwork which belongs distinctively to each of the rest."[3] The contradiction in terms in the above passage is characteristic of the writer and his school of thought. Such a subjective faith, which, as shown above, claims in the spiritual sphere to be objective, is destructive of all sense of responsibility; neither credit nor blame may be awarded to those who are not in the position to form an independent judgment of the

[1] *K.C.S. in England*, vol. i., p. 173.

[2] Mozoomdar, p. 62. [3] *Ibid.*, pp. 72-73.

spiritually "objective" revelation of God, because their own subjective faith is itself the outcome of that revelation. "We deserve," says the same writer, "no credit for (the) existence (of our church) for its success, for its influence—neither do we deserve any discredit for the singularities, accidents and dangers that have befallen the Samaj at different times."[1] Man's 'free-will' and consequent responsibility is implicitly denied.

The Third Article is one of supreme importance as defining the attitude of the Brahmo Samaj of India towards Christ. It clearly places Him on a level with other great religious teachers, and denies His Divinity in any sense other than that which may be admitted in the case of every human being. We have already pointed out what, in our opinion, has been the cause of this failure to recognize the unique character and position of Christ, viz. the wholly subjective view of Divine Revelation. The value to the members of this Samaj of every event in the world's history is its moral lesson; they look for nothing but moral teaching; their life and well-being can, they think, be affected only through their power of spiritual perception. Thus every occurrence in our Lord's life is regarded simply as an object-lesson, as moral teaching in the form of events; to the wise man, the outward form

[1] Mozoomdar, p. 355.

is of little or no importance, so long as he grasps the inward truth which it is intended to convey; facts, as such, are in themselves illusive, only means to an end; the teaching they convey is real and eternal. We feel that we are here under the influence of the doctrine of Maya, 'illusion,'[1] which gives birth to external forms with the purpose of imparting the Truth. In such an atmosphere as this we do not wonder that the fact of our Lord's resurrection from the dead fails to appeal to men as evidence of His unique relation to God, for it is regarded simply as another moral lesson on a par with those of other teachers, which took no objective form.

It will be well to give some examples to illustrate the teaching of the Samaj from which the above conclusions have been drawn. Of the later development of this society, Keshab wrote: "It is subjective; it endeavours to convert outward facts and characters into facts of consciousness; . . . (it believes that God is an objective reality)."[2] "Jesus is . . . simply a spirit to be loved, a spirit of obedience to God that must be incorporated in our spiritual being."[3] "Jesus Christ, truly analyzed, means love of God and love of man."[4] "When

[1] Sir Alfred Lyall, *Asiatic Studies*, 2nd series, p. 93; M. Müller, *Vedanta Philosophy*, p. 130.

[2] *Brahmo Year Book for* 1881, p. 43.

[3] *K.C.S. in England*, vol. i., p. 173.

[4] *Ibid.*, p. 169.

I talk of Christ, I mean simply the spirit of loyalty to God, the spirit of absolute determinedness and preparedness to say at all times and in all circumstances 'Thy will, not mine, be done.'"[1] "The true Christ of all Nations is not the Christ of flesh and blood that lived some time ago . . . not the visible, but the spiritual Christ."[2] "Must a visible Incarnation be worshipped because men cannot realize the Invisible God? God forbid! He needs not flesh to reveal Himself; He is present, filling the whole universe, one vast spiritual entity, before whose reality the world is but a delusion."[3] "He who does not understand God cannot understand Christ."[4] "True incarnation simply means God manifest in humanity; not God made man, but God *in* man."[5]

In the Fourth Article we have the claim of the Brahmo Samaj of India to Catholicity; so far as this term means the power to appeal to all classes of men we may admit the claim; but if the term be taken to mean not only the preaching to all men but also the setting forth of all truth,[6] we do not think their claim can be substantiated, The Brahmo Samaj of India by recognizing the

[1] *K.C.S. in England*, p. 176. [2] *Ibid.*, vol. ii., p. 194.

[3] *Ibid.*, vol. ii., p. 195. Note specially the reference to the "World" as "delusion."

[4] *Ibid.*, p. 196. [5] Mozoomdar, p. 374.

[6] *Pearson on the Creed*, p. 612, and Westcott, *Historic Faith*, pp. 122-3.

place of the emotions in religion had advanced beyond the Adi Brahmo Samaj whose sphere was limited by its narrow intellectualism,[1] because the former could appeal to all classes of men; but it is one thing to arouse the interest and to gain the sympathy of all men, it is quite a different thing to maintain that interest, and secure that sympathy by continually satisfying the requirements of intellect and feeling; it is here that we see the failure of the Brahmo Samaj of India; its foundation is too narrow for stability, the appeal to reason and feeling alone as final cannot satisfy those who have before them the external evidence of history.

Its claim to combine within itself the essence of all religions gives to the Brahmo Samaj of India at least the semblance of eclecticism, and having in our minds the failure of the Eclectic Reformers, Kabir and Nanak (see pp. 36 *sq.*), we cannot think that success awaits such a system; but the charge

[1] We find an illustration of the unreadiness of Unitarians to admit 'feeling' as a factor in the formation of judgment in *Dr. Lant Carpenter's Biography*, p. 238. We are told that he would not argue with his friend who had departed from Unitarian doctrine because the latter's action was due to 'feeling.' For the independent character of æsthetic feeling see Balfour *Foundations of Belief*, pp. 65-66, 326. He claims for it that "It is at least something other than the chance play of subjective sensibility or the far-off echo of ancestral lusts," nor are we "precluded . . . from referring our feeling [of beauty] to God, nor from supposing that in the thrill of some deep emotion we have for an instant caught a far-off reflection of Divine Beauty."

of eclecticism is met by the leaders of this Society[1] with a fresh definition of the word; eclecticism, they say, is taken by the Brahmos to mean not the "collection" but the *unification* of truth.[2] The work of this Samaj is further stated to be "heedful (observance) of the peculiarities of other systems of faith, and (acceptance of) every one of those peculiarities, (accumulation of) them, (assimilation of) them with its own life, and (preservation of) them in the midst of its own being."[3] The distinction between the 'collection' and the 'unification' of truth appears to us to be that in the former we have various sides of truth placed in juxtaposition to one another, without any attempt being made to destroy the distinctive character of each representation of truth; whereas the "unification" of truth implies the reduction of all sides of truth to a common denominator, this being an advance upon the collection of truth and being necessarily dependent upon it; those who claim to 'unify' truth cannot deny having already undertaken the preliminary step of 'collecting' truth. The common denominator adopted by earlier Eclectic Reformers was the acceptance of certain intellectual general principles, that which the Brahmo Samaj of India adopts is (mystic) spiritual unity; in this it finds the 'harmony of all religious dis-

[1] Mozoomdar, pp. 154 *sq.* [2] *Ibid.*, pp. 158, 173. [3] *Ibid.*, p. 161.

pensations.'[1] Can we accept such a common denominator? Its acceptance implies that reduction of objective facts to subjective interpretation, which we have already spoken of and which, as we have seen, deprives us of any criterion of truth external to ourselves. Such 'unification' of truth is worth very little when gained at the expense of truth. The following 'recommendation' of the Brahmo Samaj of India by one of its friends instances that neglect of historical evidence above referred to. "(This) reform," he says, "(is) no restoration appealing to recognized historical authority, but a movement creative of faith 'de novo.' It (does) not derive itself from the ancient religion of the country, nor from Christianity, but commence(s) afresh from the native resources of the human heart and soul."[2]

This spiritual interpretation taking the place of the simple acceptance of historic facts has had the result of raising the religion of the Brahmos above the concerns of this world; even such a petition as "Give us this day our daily bread" is to be taken as referring to spiritual food; "what is it," asked Keshab Chunder Sen, "we should pray for? Not for rain . . . not for outward prosperity

[1] Mozoomdar, p. 165.

[2] *K.C.S. in England*, vol. i., p. 12. Speech by the Rev. J. Martineau.

. . . (but) that we may enjoy . . sweet communion with the Lord. . . Let us leave all these issues (*i.e.* material blessings) in the hands of Providence."[1] So too Pertab C. Mozoomdar "there is only one prayer which we know . . "Lord, pour into my heart Thy Spirit;"[2] "The Brahmo Samaj (of India) believes in the duty and utmost efficacy of prayer for spiritual things and not for material benefits."[3] Whilst we fully admit that conformity to the will of God is the essence of prayer, we cannot but think that a religion that does not encourage prayer for material things is unsuited for those whose home, though for a time only, is in a material world.

The 5th Article enumerated above deals with sin, its consequences, and its remedy. In the recognition of the grave character of sin we see an advance upon the teaching of the Adi Brahmo Samaj (*vid.* p. 68). "In neither Ram Mohun Roy nor in Debendra Nath Tagore do we perceive the strong sense of sin, the need of regenerate life, the passionate thirst for God as Saviour and Comforter."[4] "(In 1865) for the first time in connection with the Brahmo Samaj was witnessed the rare spectacle of sinful men, *bitterly* conscious of their sins, praying and listening with living

[1] *K.C.S. in England*, vol. i., p. 69.

[2] Mozoomdar, p. 54.

[3] *Ibid.*, p. 185.

[4] *Brahmo Year Book for* 1877, p. 17; Slater, p. 136, Keshab is quoted as writing: "Sin is *not* accidental, sin is radical."

sincerity for their souls' *salvation.*"[1] In our examination of the doctrine of the Brahmo Samaj of India on sin it will be necessary clearly to define the terms used. By 'sin' we mean the assertion of our will against the will of God, or in other words, 'conscious rebellion against that which we know to be right.'[2] 'A sin' or 'sins' are actions of this nature; the result of these actions is the confirmation of the habit of opposing God, the strengthening of the bonds by which we are held; the result of sins is sin, and sin being lawlessness, it involves the punishment that accrues to every infraction of law. By the forgiveness of sins we mean the annulling of their results, it may be through suffering, so that the moral character of those who have been affected actively or passively by a sin be not thereby adversely affected, but be conformed more entirely to the will of God. The forgiveness of sins means the reversal of their results. In the Brahmo statement of doctrine concerning sin, we notice, firstly, that the results of sins rest upon those who commit them, there is no vicarious suffering;[3] and, secondly, that by effort on the part of the sinner, under

[1] *Brahmo Year Book for* 1877, p. 18; the italics are Miss Collet's.

[2] *Lectures on Church Doctrine*, Dr. Cunningham on "Sin"; Dale, *The Atonement*, p. 330.

[3] "Every sinner must suffer the consequences of his own sins sooner or later."

God's blessing, he may gain his soul's salvation, by which last term we understand the annihilation of sin. Let us notice the difficulties in which this doctrine involves us when 'sin,' 'sins,' and 'forgiveness' are given the meaning assigned to them in our definitions. Assuming, what we think will in these days be readily granted, the 'solidarity' of the human race not only in their physical but also in their spiritual nature, the objections raised against 'vicarious' suffering will bear but little weight except as against a crude misinterpretation of that term. But if 'none of us liveth to himself,' neither sinneth any to himself, and this truth must be taken account of in any doctrine of sin. Even supposing that a man could by sorrow and repentance, faith, and effort totally efface the effect for evil upon his own character of some sin, and thereby make any 'forgiveness' external to himself unnecessary, yet his efforts could not annul, still less reverse, the results in others of his sinful action; his sin continues to bear fruit, the burden of responsibility for past sin daily grows heavier; the power of blotting out the past is not his, for the taint is upon others than himself. Were it possible to think that the whole human race would as one man turn to repentance it might be possible to conceive of forgiveness of sins upon earth apart from any special dispensation, but we cannot entertain such a possibility, for we have not the slightest evidence of such general repentance in the past. The world, to find the forgiveness of sins, needs a representative man, one whose actions may be claimed as their own by all who are willing to become morally and spiritually one with him. In the Person of the Son of Man, of Jesus Christ, we see the forgiveness of sins made possible, because the sins of the world, which were the cause of His Passion and Death, became through Him motives towards obedience and love of God, instead of being fruitful in disobedience and hatred.[1] Through the action of Christ even the sins of men are made instruments of service to God; they have led to the supreme revelation of His love.[2] Jesus Christ by identifying Himself with sinners was able to offer even their past opposition, their sins, as a sacrifice to God, when in loving obedience He offered Himself. In the Crucified

[1] Dale, *The Atonement*, p. 346. God's hostility to our sins has received adequate expression in the death of Christ, and now He is ready to confer on us the remission of sins for Christ's sake.

[2] Romans iii. 5-7; Dale, *The Atonement*, p. 392. "The principle that suffering—suffering of the most terrible kind—is the just desert of sin, is not suppressed. It would have been adequately asserted had God inflicted on man the penalties of transgression. It is asserted in a still grander form and by a Divine act, which in its awful sublimity and unique glory infinitely transcends the mere infliction of suffering on those who have sinned." Westcott, *Gospel of the Resurrection*, pp. 145, 146.

and Risen Christ we have the strong assurance of the forgiveness of sins; apart from Him we cannot see even the possibility of such.

Having inquired into its fundamental teaching, we now resume once more our narrative of the Brahmo Samaj of India. After the separation of the followers of Keshab Chunder Sen from the Adi Brahmo Samaj, the former were for many months on the verge of religious despair, having no foundation on which to ground their belief, no leader and guide to encourage them to advance;[1] in 1867 Keshab was informed by his disciples that "unless there was a New Dispensation the Samaj could not be saved; unless there was a new agency to keep (them) together there would be another rupture in the Brahmo Samaj."[2] Under this pressure Keshab gave himself up to prayer and to the exercise of his spiritual powers; to such a height of spiritual enthusiasm did he attain that his followers more than regained their former confidence in him, and the Samaj received a new lease of life. Yet its stability was not ensured, for it rested upon the individuality of its leader and upon New Dispensations granted from time to time. If its leader should disappoint them by personal inconsistency, or if he should fail to usher in a New Dispensation when the enthusiasm of his disciples

[1] Mozoomdar, pp. 207-9. [2] *Ibid.*, pp. 213-4.

began to wane, the society was doomed to division and failure. These two dangers threatened the Samaj, and it was not long before it fell a victim to the former of them. One of the means by which Keshab Chunder Sen strengthened the Samaj, whilst at the same time doing really effective work, was his social reforms; through these he enlisted the sympathies of many who would not have been attracted by the directly spiritual side of his work. The most important result of these efforts was the passing in 1872 of the "Native Marriage Act," which introduced for the first time the institution of civil marriage into Hindu society.[1] It also fixed the minimum age for a bridegroom at 18 and for a bride at 14. Only six years later Keshab Chunder Sen committed the fatal mistake of ignoring the law which he had himself been instrumental in passing; he permitted the marriage of his daughter, below the age of fourteen, to the young Maharajah of Kuch Behar, who was not then sixteen years of age. As the defenders of this action have declared that what took place in 1878 was a betrothal only and not a marriage, it is well to insert here the account given of the event by the *Indian Mirror*, the Brahmo Samaj organ, and the mouthpiece of Keshab himself, in its issue of December 29,

[1] *R.A.S. Journal, cit. supra*, pp. 30-31; Mozoomdar, pp. 294-5; Slater, p. 86.

1878. "The principal event of the year was the Rajah's marriage, which was celebrated on the 6th of March. . . . It was necessary to the legality of the marriage that the rites should be Hindu in all essential features. After much deliberation and argument Babu Keshab Chunder Sen was brought to see that . . . . it was absolutely essential that the marriage . . . . should be a Hindu marriage." "The marriage has since been formally declared legal by the Commissioner, acting under Government . . . ."[1] The result of this marriage was the defection from the Brahmo Samaj of India of a large number of its members, who with the support of the Adi Brahmo Samaj organized yet a new Samaj under the title the "Sadharan" or "General" Samaj. Corresponding to this defection there was a fresh development of spiritual fervour in the Brahmo Samaj of India which to some extent counteracted the influence of the seceders. Keshab and his followers defended the Kuch Behar marriage by asserting the doctrine of special inspiration,[2] and, by adopting the phraseology of the Vaishnavites, made their teaching attractive to a far larger circle than heretofore; this last phase removes the Brahmo Samaj of India further

[1] *R.A.S. Journal*, vol. xiii., part ii., April 1881, p. 286.

[2] *Brahmo Year Book for* 1878, p. 36; Slater, p. 86; Bhattacharjee, pp. 159-171.

from Christianity, and from pure monotheism. We shall therefore not follow its history further, but content ourselves with noticing those aspects of its teaching which have not yet come before us, and with estimating the strength and the weakness of this Samaj as a factor in the development of the religious life of India.

We have already said something of the advance which the Brahmo Samaj of India made upon the teaching of the Adi Brahmo Samaj in its recognition of the place in true religion of the emotions as well as of the reason; its leaders saw that a faith incapable of kindling enthusiasm was powerless to control the lives of those who professed it; they recognized the truth so well expressed by a great Englishman, "No heart is pure that is not passionate; no virtue is safe that is not enthusiastic."[1] "How can I be free," asks Pertab C. Mozoomdar, "from the carnal passions of my own nature unless there is a more powerful passion to hold them down, and to turn them from evil into good?"[2] We see also a corresponding advance in another direction; the Brahmo Samaj of India felt the need in the Object of their worship of a Personality corresponding to the Personality of Man; they did not rest satisfied in an Abstract Idea[3] however beautiful it

[1] Sir John Seeley, *Ecce Homo*, p. 8. [2] Mozoomdar, p. 59.

[3] *Ibid.*, pp. 91, 179; *Keshab C. Sen in England*, vol. i., pp. 40 *sq.*

might be; in this yearning after God revealed perfectly in man we recognize a testimony to the truth, and evidence of Christ's being "The Desire of All Nations"; yet no sooner did this yearning take definite form and seem about to be satisfied in the person of Jesus Christ than it was negatived by the mysticism which loves to explain away the facts of history.[1] The human centre of the Christian faith was recognized to be its strength, yet the leaders of the Brahmo Samaj of India would not commit themselves to the acceptance of the God-Man.[2] In the words of a Christian poet we find at once the expression of the need that gave birth to this Samaj, and the assurance which they yet seek that that need has been met in an historic character. "'Tis the weakness in strength that I cry for, my flesh that I seek in the Godhead! I seek and I find it. O Saul, it shall be a Face like my face that receives thee, a Man like to me, thou shalt love and be loved by for ever; a Hand like this hand shall throw open the gates of new life to thee! See the Christ stand!"[3]

[1] *Vide* Slater, appendix, p. 107; Robson, *Hinduism and Christianity*, pp. 279 *seq.*

[2] *Ibid.*, pp. 142-4, 102-3; *R.A.S. Journal*, Jan. 1881, p. 37. "It is evident that Mr. Sen intends Christ to be accepted by his fellow-countrymen as the greatest of all Asiatic saints, and not in the character ascribed to Him by the Church of England"; *R.A.S. Journal*, 1881, p. 288.

[3] R. Browning, *Saul*, xviii.

As a witness to truths ignored by earlier Theistic reformers, we value highly the Brahmo Samaj of India, but its lack of an historic basis has, we think, already proved, and will, till remedied, ever prove fatal to the society. Its emotionalism knows no bounds; it carries us beyond the laws of moral right and wrong laid down for the government of man; "true Bhakti is beyond the region of morality and immorality;"[1] by ignoring the distinction between the finite and the infinite, between God and man, the reverence that is due to God is lost, and we find terms of endearment applied to Him that seem calculated to destroy any conception of awe in the presence of His unapproachable holiness.[2] Its emotionalism has given rise to the doctrine of the maternity of God, as more calculated to stir the emotions than the belief in His Fatherhood,[3] and also to the resuscitation of the idolatrous worship of Hari.[4] Christianity on

[1] Mozoomdar, p. 338. [The whole context should be read to avoid possible misrepresentation. The essayist does not agree with Mozoomdar in thinking that the danger of immorality is removed from him who is admitted to Bhakti.]

[2] *K.C.S. in England*, vol. i., p. 88, "Oh, I wish I could hug my God to my heart"; vol. ii., p. 200, "My God is a sweet God."

[3] Mozoomdar, pp. 394-401; Slater, pp. 97-99; *Brahmo Year Book for* 1879, p. 31. *The Sunday Mirror*, speaking of a missionary expedition, says, "'The mother, the mother, the mother'—this is the battle-cry with which the expedition has fought."

[4] *Brahmo Year Book for* 1880, pp. 32 and 33—citations from the *The Sunday Mirror*: "The Brahmo Samaj preaches no idolatry, no

the contrary has been safeguarded against such a relapse into heathen mythology and spiritual extravagance by the appeal of eye-witnesses to the historic facts which it was their mission to proclaim; if the Brahmo Samaj of India is to save the people of the country which by its title it claims to represent, it must listen to, and then make its own the assertion of the foundation in the life of the world of the revelation it proclaims. They will have a gospel to deliver, as well as an ideal to depict, when they can say with St. John, "The Word became flesh and dwelt amongst us, and we beheld His glory," and when they can proclaim Him "Who has been seen with the eyes, and felt with the hands,"[1] as being in a unique sense the Son of God.

mediation, no miracles, no creed-bound faith. All its changes are wrung upon that single word—God-Mother. . . . It is a great consolation to think that at anyrate above 12,000 people seriously heard the name of Hari during the past fortnight. . . . We have found out that every idol worshipped by the Hindus represents an attribute of God, and that each attribute is called by a particular name."

[1] 1 John i. 3; Trench, *Hulsean Lectures*, pp. 198-9: "A system which shrinks from saying 'Christ is God' finds it impossible to rest in that denial . . . and hasten(s) to say 'Man is God,' giving in the end to every man that which it started with affirming it was blasphemy to give to any, even to the Son Himself."

THE SADHARAN BRAHMO SAMAJ.

THE schism in the Brahmo Samaj of India which led to the formation of the Sadharan Brahmo Samaj was due, as we have seen, to the action of Keshab Chunder Sen in regard to his daughter's marriage. The confidence of the Samaj in their leader being thus rudely shaken, many of its members felt it necessary to reconsider their position and the organization of the Society, the result being that they determined in future to have a representative government, and no longer to be dominated by the influence of one man however commanding his genius might be. There is little doubt that this realization of the need of a constitutional government of the Samaj was due to their acquaintance with the Christian Church, the stability and world-wide influence of which had deeply impressed them for they seem to have attributed the strength of the Christian Church to its organization as such rather than to its foundation upon the historic and living Christ.[1]

An attempt was made to call a general meeting of the Brahmo Samaj of India to reconsider the whole question of its organization, but this failed owing to the secretary's (Pertab C. Mozoomdar, a strong supporter of Keshab Chunder Sen) very tardy acquiescence in the request, though made by a large majority of the branches of the Samaj.[2] The seceders accordingly, under the leadership of Ananda Mohan Bose, held an independent meeting at Calcutta on May 15, 1878, at which they had the support of the Adi Brahmo Samaj and its venerable head, Debendra Nath Tagore. The meeting deplored the want of a constitutional basis in the Brahmo Samaj of India and established the Sadharan Brahmo Samaj. The new Samaj proclaimed as its object the 'realization of the grand ideal of Rammohun Roy, from which (they said) the Brahmos had greatly departed.'[3] Truths were to be collected from all the teachers and all the scriptures of all countries.[4] Although the difference between the Brahmo Samaj of India and the Sadharan Brahmo Samaj was primarily one of organization, it necessarily entailed differences of

[1] Mozoomdar, pp. 140 *sq.*; *R.A.S. Journal*, Jan. 1881, pp. 37-38; Slater, pp. 86-87.

[2] *Brahmo Year Book for* 1878, p. 73.

[3] *Brahmo Year Book for* 1881, p. 71.

[4] *Ibid.*, for 1879, p. 75.

creed because the creed of the former Samaj was, to so great an extent, coloured by the personal predilections of its founder. In the fact that the Sadharan Samaj promulgated a new creed, we have evidence which proves to how small an extent the creed of Keshab Chunder Sen was the creed of those who professed to be his followers; the Christianity of the Brahmo Samaj of India was less than skin deep. It remains for us to examine the creed put forward by the Sadharan Brahmo Samaj. This creed is a development of that of the Adi Brahmo Samaj as formulated by Debendra Nath Tagore.[1] and the criticism passed upon it above (pp. 69-76) will apply also to the creed now before us, we need therefore deal only with the developments of the latter. These are chiefly of a negative character and directly opposed to that Christian teaching which Keshab Chunder Sen claimed to assimilate to his own doctrines. The most important article is the following: "We regard the belief in an individual being a way to salvation, or a link between God and man, as a belief unworthy of a Theist, and those who hold such a belief as unworthy of the Brahmo name."[2] This statement of belief is made yet more explicit in the words of the leaders of this Samaj. Thus S. K. Chatterji, in a lecture in 1879, said, "Theists

[1] Slater, pp. 94-95. [2] *Brahmo Year Book for* 1878, pp. 74-75.

(can) never accept Christ (as the Saviour of mankind, the mediator between God and man) as they inculcate direct communion and relationship between God and man; they (are) in need of no mediator." "India does not want Christ for her salvation. . . . The Theistic religion of India is in no way inferior to the teachings of the Bible—the Vedas and the Upanishads (are) sufficient for our salvation." "There was no more divinity in (Christ) than what every man has."[1] Another member of the same Samaj is yet more extreme in his views, and his words suggest the reckless acceptance of statements of the opponents of Christianity, without a careful study of the history of that faith; "even granting," says Sivanath Sastri, "that such a being (as Christ) ha(s) existed, there have been men among His followers superior to Him in many respects.[2]

The following extract from a sermon preached at the Anniversary of the Sadharan Brahmo Samaj in 1880 will suffice to express the doctrinal attitude of the Society: "God never forsakes men." "(This) means that God is always AFTER US" . . . "The doctrine is not at all new. What, for instance, is the doctrine of Incarnation, believed by the orthodox portion of our countrymen, and by whole Christendom? The cardinal point in such a

[1] *Brahmo Year Book for* 1879, p. 77. [2] *Ibid.*, p. 78.

doctrine is the idea that God comes down to help humanity . . . Man surely needs a lifting power . . . a force coming from without. This power is in God and from God it must be communicated to the soul of man. For the purpose of such communication it is not needful that God should suffer the bonds of flesh. . . . on the side of God there is no slackness of pursuit, but it is we, who do not bend the knees of our proud will before His redeeming grace."[1]

Much as we may value the above statement as a true expression of the yearning love of God for His children, we cannot shut our eyes to the fact that in other respects the doctrine of the Samaj is totally at variance with Christian truth. The differences between us are fundamental; we not only draw opposite conclusions, but we draw them from different premises. Until our premises be granted we cannot therefore enter into argument with any hope of attaining to the unity of faith.[2] Because they are drawn from the experience of life, so long as our experience is different, so too will be our religious premises. We Christians claim to possess a more comprehensive experience,

[1] *Ibid.* for 1880, p. 14.

[2] "All moral reasoning must ultimately rest on the internal evidence of the moral sense; and when this is disordered, the most unquestionable logic can conclude nothing, because it is the first principles which are at issue."—James Spedding on *The Two Voices.* Tennyson, *Life*, vol. i., p. 193.

that of all men, at all times, and under all conditions of life.[1] We consider the position of Theism to be impregnable so long as those who maintain it separate themselves from the life of the world, and ignore its facts; but if they mix with all classes of society, the rich and the poor, the religious and the irreligious, we maintain that they must recognize the need of a Human Saviour, for they will see the repeated failure of the highest spiritual teaching, by itself, to raise men,[2] and they will also see countless human beings saved by the personal influence of men whose doctrine is absorbed in character.[3] This fact, that personal human influence is the greatest moral force, leads us to look for the closest union with God through this means; our experience of life prepares us to come to God through a Human-Divine Mediator. As Man He draws us, as God He raises us; God and Man being One Person in Christ, devotion to Jesus spells love of God, and love of God becomes a power within us even in this world.[4]

[1] See V. H. Stanton, *Place of Authority*, pp. 53 *sq.*, with his criticism of J. S. Mill, on the argument *e consensu omnium*. Trench, *Hulsean Lectures*, 1846, pp. 225-6: "They are as busy about sacrifices in the outer Court of the Gentiles as in the Holier Place of the Jews."

[2] Even Muhammedanism is now in part bearing witness to this truth; the sect of the Shiaks celebrate the death of Hussein as one who died for the sins of the whole world. *Vid.* C. M. S., *Gleaner*, Aug., 1900, p. 124.

[3] Trench, *Hulsean Lectures*, 1846, p. 262.

[4] *Ibid.*, pp. 167-70 and pp. 192-4.

THE ARYA SAMAJ.

We have already seen how the Brahmo Samaj of Calcutta, under the Presidency of Debendra Nath Tagore, rejected the doctrine of the infallible inspiration of the Vedas, and thus departed from one of the main principles (see p. 68) laid down by the founder of the society. Through this great crisis the Samaj passed without an open schism, the majority being on the side of the new doctrine, and the minority giving way to them. But belief in the infallibility of the Vedas and their sufficiency through all time, to salvation, had not been finally destroyed. It was revived by Dayananda Sarasvati, who founded a society entitled the Arya Samaj; to him the Vedas were the only Revelation, and when freed from later accretions, and interpreted according to his own canon of interpretation, absolutely infallible.[1] His conception of God was of One abstracted from all idea of shape and

[1] Slater, pp. 37-38; *R.A.S. Journal*, Jan., 1881, pp. 40-41; Oman, pp. 113-114; Max Müller, *Biographical Essays*; Dayananda, p. 170.

form without any second, as set forth in the Vedas. He rejected the doctrine of the personality of God, because to him this meant earthly, material, limitations.[1] He endeavoured to show that the Vedas condemn idolatry, and teach all science.[2] His followers maintain that every part of the Vedas (proper) is written in the name of the whole, *i.e.* represents the whole inspired book, and is not the expression of this or that, probably mistaken, individual.[3] The character of the Founder of this Samaj was very different from that of the noble Rammohun Roy, the conscientious Debendra Nath, and the enthusiastic Keshab Chunder Sen; he seems to have been, by his own admission, both untruthful and addicted to intoxication.[4] It is evident that we have now before us a question totally different from that raised by the Brahmo Samaj; this is not so much a question of ethics, religion, and philosophy, as of literary criticism. Can the assertion by the Arya Samaj of the unity of the Vedas, and their pure monotheistic teaching, be substantiated? The question can be answered only by Sanskrit scholars, and

[1] Oman, p. 105.

[2] T. Williams, *Three Letters, an Exposure of Dayananda Sarasvati*, Delhi, 1889; Oman, pp. 113-115; Dr. Martyn Clark, *Lecture* i., p. 5; *Lecture* iv., p. 3.

[3] T. Williams, 2nd Letter.

[4] Oman, pp. 106-110, with citations from the *Theosophist*.

to them we must refer the matter. Dayananda's renderings of certain passages have been challenged; he is said to have materially changed the meaning by deliberately misrepresenting person, mood, and conjugation.[1] Into the larger questions we have already enquired (pp. 11 *sq.*), with the result that we find in the Mantras Henotheism[2] rather than Monotheism, and in the Upanishads, a further development in the direction of pure Monotheism, but a Monotheism so vague as to be constantly lapsing into Pantheism. We cannot therefore accept the first principles of this Samaj nor regard it as building upon any sure foundation; yet, because in India the creations of Illusion are forces that cannot be ignored, it is well that we should go a little further and enquire into the practical character and influence of the Arya Samaj at the present time.

Consistently with their adherence to Vedic teaching, the members of the Arya Samaj on special occasions duly perform the "Hom" sacrifice. Pieces of dry wood are arranged in the form of a square sacrificial pit; at each corner of this is placed a composition of fragrant and combustible gums, and around them

[1] T. Williams, 1st and 2nd Letters. Yet Dayananda has the reputation amongst his fellow-countrymen of being 'the greatest Vedic scholar of the age.' Oman, p. 91, *Cit. Civil and Military Gazette*, March 6, 1879.

[2] Müller, *cit.* Oman, p. 115.

are placed four brass vessels containing spices and grain, and a fifth vessel containing clarified butter (ghee). The firewood and resinous gums are lighted and the flames are fed from the contents of the five vessels, during which ceremony Mantras are recited in Sanskrit by the officiating priest.[1] In this manner the ancient Vedic sacrifice to Agni is maintained; but although this practice is the logical outcome of their adherence to the Vedas, many members of the Arya Samaj find in it a stumbling-block; they do not know what attitude to assume with regard to it; on the one hand the influence of Western thought has destroyed their faith in the efficacy of such a sacrifice, on the other hand the spirit of conservatism and their obligation to follow the teaching of the Vedas prevents their ignoring the sacrifice altogether. The practical consequence is this, that some members of the Samaj declare the purpose of the ceremony to be scientific fumigation for sanitary reasons, whilst others take the middle course of giving their support to those who offer the sacrifice by their presence at the service, whilst they exonerate themselves from any charge of idolatrous worship by studied carelessness and inattention during the performance of the rites.[2] We cannot but regard such an attitude as this as being

[1] Oman, pp, 88, 95, and 96.

[2] Oman, pp. 79, 101, 102. Dr. Martyn Clark, *Lecture VI.*, p. 2 *sqq.*

temporary.[1] On the one side the old faith has been destroyed; on the other a new and living faith, that of Christianity, is being introduced into the country. Were it not for the latter it is probable that we should see no attempt to revive the old faith; we may regard the existence of the Arya Samaj as to a large extent the result of Christian missions; and so far as open antagonism is less bad than sullen indifference, the result is one for which we may be thankful.[2] The Arya Samaj, out of patriotic antagonism to Christianity,[3] has assumed a position which is becoming more and more clearly untenable; there seems good reason to believe that as Christianity is shown to be a universal and not merely a national faith, the prejudices which have given birth to the Arya Samaj will die, and its antagonism to Christianity will cease. At the present time the cause of the Arya Samaj is promoted by charges against Christians of ignoring the Hindụ Scriptures, of circulating the Bible by

[1] Bp. Lightfoot, *Christianity and Paganism*, pp. 87, 95, 96.

[2] *Delhi Mission Report*, 1898, p. 37. "They openly declare themselves to be enemies of ours, and deny the possibility of the Incarnation, but they acknowledge more frankly than most the sinfulness of men and the need of strenuous efforts to obtain salvation."

[3] Oman, pp. 120-121. *Delhi Mission Report*, 1898, pp. 38-39. "In Rohtak itself a branch of the Arya Samaj has been established, which I cannot help looking upon as an indirect result of our work. . . . I believe that it is a real move forward, and an attempt to accept Christianity without 'the offence of the cross.'"

thousands whilst only talking of getting a translation of the Vedas."[1] Such charges are being falsified by the increasing study by Europeans of the Religious Books of India, and we may hope to see religious prejudice fade away, as enlightened sympathy makes common religious thought possible. The outcome of a recent public discussion between a Christian missionary and an 'orthodox' Hindu was that members of the Arya Samaj told the former that they were satisfied in some ways at the result of the discussion, and would like to have another on their own account after having had time to think over the unfamiliar lines of argument adopted by him.[2] We see here that the members of the Arya Samaj are susceptible to argument when their prejudices are not aroused, and when they are allowed time for thought, and liberty to form their own judgment. This being the state of the Arya Samaj, of what immense importance is it that Christians should gently and tactfully break down the barrier of ignorant prejudice, both by making themselves acquainted with Indian literature and by coming, directly or through their representatives the missionaries, into sympathetic touch with these men.

[1] *Delhi Mission Report*, 1899, p. 36. [2] *Ibid.*, p. 38.

CONCLUSION.

We now approach the conclusion of our work; we have traced in outline the history in India of Theistic thought up to the time of Rammohun Roy; we have seen progress first in one direction and then in another, but in the case of every Theistic reform we have found some fundamental want or error that accounts for its failure to become universal. We have examined more closely the Theistic Reforms, which, beginning with that of Rammohun Roy, bear evident traces of the influence of Christianity, viz., the Brahmiya Samaj, the Adi Brahmo Samaj (that of Calcutta) the Brahmo Samaj of India, the Sadharan Samaj, and that which is essentially distinct from these—the Arya Samaj. We have been compelled to limit our treatment of these societies to a brief enquiry into their history and doctrine, and to pointing out what appears to us in each case to differentiate the teaching of the Samaj from that of the Christian Church, hoping thereby to make it evident what line of argument should be adopted by those who contend with them on the battlefield of India.

Thus we think that the Adi Brahmo Samaj, and the Sadharan Samaj need to have placed clearly before them the inability of man, by reason of sin, to have communion with God, and the fact that God does draw men to Himself through the personal influence of individual men, who are thus types of the unique Mediator between God and man.

In the case of the Brahmo Samaj of India we think that it can be brought into the truth only through the acceptance of sound historic principles;[1] the systematic teaching of history, especially the history of those countries where external events are seen to mould the character of nations, as in the case of the Jews,[2] will give to the Brahmo Samaj of India that sense of proportion that they at present lack, and will serve as an antidote to that narrow subjectivism which at present makes them blind to God's objective revelation in Jesus Christ.

In the Arya Samaj we have an avowed enemy, but one who appears to be susceptible to courtesy,

[1] See Sir A. Lyall, *Asiatic Studies*, 2nd series, pp. 88-89, where a Hindu defends the principle of dissolving history into mysticism. Westcott, *Gospel of the Resurrection*, p. 52, § 9, "The doctrines of Christianity flow from alleged facts. The belief in the historic event precedes the belief in the dogma."

[2] G. A. Smith, *Historical Geography of Palestine*, p. 33.

and likely to become Christian when the increase of knowledge, and the brotherly love of Christians has warmed their hearts and enlightened their minds. Their position is, in the face of modern literary criticism, so obviously untenable, that if we make it possible for them to evacuate it without loss of self-respect they will in all probability do so before very long, and once they are enrolled in the Christian ranks, their known conservatism will give their witness to Christ far more weight with their fellow-countrymen, than that of men regarded as reckless revolutionists and the introducers of a foreign creed.

Before we close it is right that we should seek an answer to the burning question, "What prospect is there of India as a whole accepting Christianity?" We dare not speak dogmatically on a matter on which the greatest writers are at variance; we dare not 'rush in where (scholars) fear to tread'; but it may be useful to summarize the verdicts of leading students of the subject and estimate their force from the standpoint of the Catholic Church. Twenty years ago the French writer Barth could venture on no answer as to the future faith of India; to him Christian missionary enterprize seemed to fail owing to the too great use of argument; the solution must come through life rather than through abstract thought.[1] We find more encouragement when we turn to a recent work also entitled *The Religions of India.* Professor Hopkins points out that the comparative failure of Christianity in the past to become the religion of India has been greatly due to the open antagonism between its doctrines and the lives of those who profess them. "Not the heathen, but the Christian, barred the way against Christianity. . . . The hand stole and killed; the mouth said, 'I love you.' The Hindoo understood theft and murder, but it took him some time to learn English. All this must be remembered when the expenditures of Christianity are weighed with its receipts."[2] The character of Christian influence in India is now quite other than it was, and the chief barrier to advance is being broken down. The same writer recommends the preaching of the simplest creed, and the precept both in word and life "Thou shalt love the Lord thy God, and thy neighbour as thyself," and is able to see in the distant future the rise of a spirit of progress which will set India free to accept Christ.[3] Another witness to the future progress of Christianity in India is Sir Monier Monier Williams, who, in his comparison of the religions of India, is able to say that "the masses (of India) will never be satisfied with (Positivism).

[1] Barth, pp. 28-9, *sq.* [2] Hopkins, pp. 565-6. [3] *Ibid.*, pp. 570-1.

Christianity has many more points of contact with their ancient faith than Islam has; and when the walls of the mighty fortress of Brahmanism are encircled, undermined, and finally stormed by the soldiers of the Cross, the victory of Christianity must be signal and complete."[1] Turning to other evidence, we are told that Brahmanism is at present absorbing many who otherwise would accept Christianity or Islam;[2] it recognizes with sympathy some of the needs of men, and by its sympathy secures their adherence to its principles, and unconsciously keeps them back from that faith which not only recognizes but also satisfies all human needs; this is a fact which shows the importance of immediate effort being made to present the Gospel of Christ to all the aboriginal tribes of India before they are drawn into the maze of Brahmanism. As to Brahmanism itself, the same writer thinks that it, in a simplified form, will be the religion of the masses for generations to come,[3] and that in the far future we may look to see prevalent in India a narrow egotism, without religion, and without reason, and nothing but confusion and distress.[4] And yet beyond this again he sees the establishment of one religious system, for which the way will have been prepared by the unifying

[1] M. Williams, *Modern India* (1878).

[2] Sir A. Lyall, 1st Series, p. 108. [3] *Ibid.*, p. 119. [4] *Ibid.*, p. 121.

influence of British rule; that faith, he thinks, may possibly be Islam.[1]

The above citations suffice to exemplify the greatly varying interpretations of the signs of the times; the character of each interpretation corresponds to the position assumed by each interpreter. Those who refrain from taking part in the active propagation of the Christian faith, assuming an attitude of strict neutrality, can see only a field for doubtful speculation; whereas those who identify themselves with Christian missionary enterprize are able to entertain the assured belief that India is being rapidly prepared for the general acceptance of Christian truth. Before we accept either interpretation we must decide which is in the best position to form a sound judgment, whether the looker-on or he who is engaged in the work; for our own part, we think that St. Paul the Missionary could have given a more accurate forecast of the future of Christianity than could the ruler Gallio, and that those who mark the effect of Christian teaching upon their own Hindu pupils are better able to gauge its power than those who judge of its future according to the rapidity with which it spreads; because Christianity demands the regeneration of each individual with the complete transformation of his character rather than the

[1] Sir A. Lyall, pp. 296 and 302.

acceptance of general truths, we think that the index to its progress is to be found within the personal experience of the individual. The general acceptance of nominal Christianity, which might lead an outside observer to comment on its success, would be to the thoughtful missionary but an illusory promise could he see nothing deeper; whereas the absence of such a general acceptance troubles him little when he knows of individuals whose lives have been transformed by the Gospel; accepting the principle that the Kingdom of God is like leaven, he looks cheerfully forward to see in due time the leavening of the whole population of the world, and in the light of this reasonable hope he interprets the signs of the times as pointing to the speedy Advent of Christ to India.